MIRACLE
FROM THE
STREETS

**Abused and unwanted,
Cheri found a life of
violence and addiction
from which she knew
there was no escape—
until she was shown
the power of God's
unconditional love.**

CHERI PETERS

Pacific Press Publishing Association
Nampa, Idaho
Oshwa, Ontario, Canada

Edited by Sophie Anderson and Kenneth R. Wade
Designed by Dennis Ferree
Cover illustration by Bryant Eastman

Copyright © 1997 by
Pacific Press Publishing Association
Printed in the United States of America
All Rights Reserved

Peters, Cheri Ann, 1955-
    A miracle from the streets / Cheri Ann Peters.
      p.   cm.
    ISBN 0-8163-1360-1 (pbk. : alk. paper)
1. Peters, Cheri Ann, 1955- . 2. Converts—United
States—Biography.   3.   Narcotic addicts—United
States—Biography.   4.   Adult child sexual abuse
victims—United States—Biography. I. Title.
BV4935.P48A3   1997
248.2'46'092—dc
[B]   96-34387
                                                                                  CIP

97 98 99 00 01 • 5 4 3 2 1

This book is dedicated to God,
whose unconditional love
continues to work miracles in my life,
and to Brad and Jacqi,
the family He has given me.

FOREWORD

To hear Cheri Peters's story is to be forever changed. To meet Cheri in person is to encounter a flesh-and-blood, bona fide miracle. To know Cheri as a personal friend is an incredible privilege—one that I am blessed to have.

Cheri blasts to smithereens the notion that the day of miracles has passed or that God's direct working in human lives ended after the apostles all died off. When you watch this denim-clad dynamo sitting cross-legged on the floor holding an audience of abused, troubled teenagers spellbound with her life story of salvation from the streets; or watch her tumble down a grassy hill laughing with childlike glee followed by a trail of squealing, tumbling preschoolers; or see her on her own television show pulling heart-rending testimonies from her guests and getting so caught up in the drama that she sometimes forgets details like commercial breaks; or hold in your hands this book, knowing that it was written by someone who at one time could barely read; it is *then* you realize that you're looking at a modern-day Lazarus. A 1990s

A MIRACLE FROM THE STREETS

Mary Magdalene. A twentieth-century Samaritan woman at the well. A living testimony of God's awesome restorative power and His amazing grace.

Between the ages of thirteen and twenty-three, Cheri Peters lived on the streets. Sexually abused by her father, unloved and rejected by her mother, she carved out a rugged existence amid urban America's teeming homeless population. This is her story—one you won't soon forget.

Cheri's life was raw, and she's made no attempt to smooth the painful edges from this narrative. It isn't prettied-up for the squeamish or spiritual sophisticates. It's a real story of what it's like to find deliverance from being hell's plaything and become a bride of Christ. It shows how God can still find beauty among the ashes and how His love can transform the straw of a broken life into pure gold.

I read in the book of Acts that to look on the face of Stephen was to look on "the face of an angel." When you talk to Cheri, you know what that radiance of Stephen's looked like. Cheri is on fire. She burns with a white-hot love for people—especially the lost and lonely—and is ablaze with the unconditional love of Christ. I, and others who know her, are ignited by her flame.

The following statement from the great prayer warrior E. M. Bounds captures both the essence of this book and the heart of its author.

> No farness to which Israel had gone, no depth to which Israel had fallen, no chains however iron with which Israel was bound but that their cry to God easily spanned the distance, fathomed the depths, and broke the chains. . . . There was nothing too hard for God to do for His people—(*The Complete Words of E. M. Bounds on Prayer* (Grand Rapids, Mich.: Baker Book House, 1990).

The Cheri Peters Story

The urgent prayer of my heart is that everyone who reads these pages will come face to face with the God who breaks the strongest chains of addiction and emotional damage; the God who easily spans the greatest distances between us; and the God for whom nothing is too hard.

It's not every day you get to encounter a miracle. Your day has come. Rejoice.

Randy Maxwell,
Author of *If My People Pray*

PROLOGUE

I heard you're writing a book." My father's mother spits over the phone.

"Yes." My pulse pounds.

"You're not writing about us! You're not writing about the time you spent here, are you?"

"Actually, I . . ."

"You shamed us. Twelve years old, pregnant. Your grandfather and I told everyone you had a kidney infection, but I know they didn't believe us. We didn't want you. I called your dad and told him never to send any more of his trampy kids to us!"

Lord, help!

"You're not mentioned. In fact, until now my memory has blocked out the time I spent with you. I've even tried to forget the death of the twins, that whole experience." Forgotten images pummel me. "Do you want to know why I was such a trampy kid? I was psychologically and sexually abused since birth. Do you think someone from a normal, loving family ends up pregnant at twelve?"

"I don't care. I don't want to know."

"But I . . ."

"But I do want you to know that you will not destroy my good name."

Her voice wrings with venom.

"I want you to know something else. Your grandfather never loved you! He finally figured out a way to send you home."

Stop, please stop! A silent scream shakes me.

"He told me over and over he wanted you out of his house." She pauses, triumphant.

He did care! Please say he cared about me. My grandfather, one of the few kind adults in my childhood, once took me fishing. Perched with me on a warm rock, he reminisced on fishing, nature, and life. Her burning words melt the memory, a Rockwell painting. The colors of that brightness bleed, leaving gray and loss.

My grandmother breaks the silence. "You say your dad molested you? If he did anything to you, it was because of his thyroid! His thyroid dropped so low he could have died. It caused him to drink heavily, and he struggled to eat or even take care of himself." *Can she, a retired nurse, really believe that?*

"I am not writing to slander anyone's character, nor to defend my innocence. You're right. I was a mess. But most of us are. I'm writing this book to tell all the messed up the news. Even though God knows everything about you, He still loves you! He wants to heal you. He'll create in you a new life, not just patch things up. He'll 'give you hope and a future' (Jer. 29:11, NIV). This book is to tell the world that my God loves even trampy kids."

Click.

CHAPTER

first saw the $86,000 in an elegant restaurant.

"Why are there no other customers?" I had asked when we first came in.

"The entire upper floor is reserved just for us," Max explained.

The restaurant, overlooking the twinkling lights of the San Francisco Bay, was plush with intricately woven carpet and red-linen tablecloths set with delicate wine crystal. Arrangements of exotic flowers hugged by dark green foliage scented each table. Ivory candlesticks, flickering soft light, glistened in the crystal place settings and silverware.

Stacked neatly among this opulence were Ziploc bags full of white powder, seven pounds of cocaine Max and I had brought from Los Angeles.

I fidgeted with my thick linen napkin. *What are we doing here?* The dish of steamed gourmet vegetables in front of me lost its appeal. Uncrossing my legs under the table, I shifted taller in my chair, trying to look natural. New men's voices entered the room, polite banter. I tensed. *We aren't going to do a drug deal here, are we?* My heart began to race. *What am I doing here? The waiters will report us. We're going to get busted. The police will break in at any time. They will think I'm involved. If we're caught, I'll be sent to jail, maybe for life. Worse, if the deal goes bad, other dealers would kill for the amount of drugs we have.* I was used to small time, back-alley crime. This was another world.

I watched as the two men, whom Max called chemists, approached with trays of chemicals. They methodically set up a variety of tubes, scales, and other drug testing paraphernalia on a nearby table. Fascinated, I stared at the process as they tested the cocaine. They were businessmen and scientists with degrees in chemistry. They knew their stuff.

"This is close to pure. It must be your personal stash," the taller of the two mused as he watched the color change to a golden brown after he dropped a few grains of cocaine and some chemicals into a test tube.

"It's the best of the best." Max smiled.

The activity intense, all eyes focused on what these two men were doing. The pricing would be done after the chemists determined the quality of the cocaine. These two men, independent contractors, made their living by testing drugs during or before major deals could be put together.

As Max proceeded to sell seven pounds of cocaine, I stared at $86,000 cash on the table and the small piles of coke. I glanced at the waiters. They hovered close, dressed in black tuxedos, refilling my wine goblet each time I gulped it dry, attentive to our every comfort. The staff treated us not like criminals, major drug dealers, but as if we were visiting celebrities. I could have been the cuisine editor from the *San Francisco Chronicle*. The incongruity of the situation was bizarre, like a twilight zone.

He's out of your league, John's warning echoed. I had met Max first in the bar where I worked as a dancer in Los Angeles.

"Come on, Cheri," John, the club owner, had said after my nine-hour shift. "There's a guy here to meet." He waved me into the back office where a drug deal was being made. A good-looking man with brown, wavy hair, a strong jawline, and flashy smile, Max notched above the crowd that frequented the club. Hip, tan, and clean, he was a drug runner for high-class attorneys in Newport Beach. Max caught my attention immediately because he was lively. We sat around smoking pot, snorting coke, and drinking tequila. We had something going.

"Are you free later?" Max had asked, his dark eyes holding mine.

"Definitely."

"He's out of your league," John told me as I walked out with my shiny man. Perhaps John was right, but I was bored with vegging out on old sofas with my old crowd. Max had money, he had drugs. In the dead atmosphere of my life, Max was fresh air. He was fun.

Now, here in the elite restaurant, cold fingers of fear slipped around me. The staff, the chemists, and the dealers obviously knew Max. No one seemed intimidated by what was going on, the amount of drugs or money on the table. No one except me. Finishing the meal, Max tipped with several grams of cocaine, his way of saying that the service had been excellent.

Max put $19,000 in his leather satchel, along with three ounces of coke for our own personal use. The rest of the coke was sold and $67,000 placed in a separate suitcase.

Then we returned to our hotel room. Max emptied the cocaine from his satchel, then counted the money again, and returned it to the satchel. He then turned to the cocaine. He brought out a small pipe, put a few grains of cocaine into it, and placed it in his mouth, inhaling deeply.

"Have you ever free-based cocaine before?" he said, still holding in the smoke.

"No. I've never *smoked* cocaine before," I blurted.

"What?" Max was incredulous. "Well, you're in for a real treat. It's an incredible high." I trembled. I had heard that freebasing cocaine was an outrageous high but the addiction was quick and fierce. I knew many girls who prostituted themselves to support this habit. Sure, I'd snorted coke before but had always avoided smoking it. I'd seen too many of my friends get trashed. Smoking coke turned a person into a scum addict quicker than snorting it. Would I have to resort to prostitution to maintain my choice? It would be downhill from here. I backed away, but Max insisted.

All night we smoked cocaine. The morning came too quickly. Though tired, we had to catch a flight back to Los Angeles. We did more coke and left for the airport.

"How do we get this on board?" I asked Max. "They're going to see this when we go through check-in." Visions of police shoving us to the wall, yelling, and handcuffing us filled me. *Someone is following us—was I just being paranoid, or was that guy, reading the newspaper, really looking at me? Hadn't I seen those two men in shades and dark suits back at the hotel?*

Max laughed at me. We checked in the suitcase with the $67,000, disguised as my suitcase, and found our seats on the plane. It didn't occur to me until later that Max had insisted that anything related to the drug deal be checked under my name. Max even had me carry the satchel onto the plane. In case of trouble, I would be the scapegoat. Once on the plane, Max relaxed, opened the satchel, and removed some coke from it.

"What are you doing?" I demanded. "Are you crazy?"

"Everything's fine," he assured me.

"Please fasten your seat belts. Make sure your tray table and seat are in their full upright and locked position," the overhead speaker droned. Max placed two long lines of cocaine on his dinner tray.

"The attendant is coming!" I protested. "Have you completely lost your . . ."

The flight attendant leaned over and snorted the cocaine.

She thanked Max, and prepared for takeoff—in more ways than one. I began to feel sick. *Was everyone wearing a mask?*

We arrived at the airport in Los Angeles without problems. I had ingested an incredible amount of drugs and alcohol and had had no sleep for three days. I felt like roadkill, smashed by the eighteen-wheeler of cocaine. More than physically flayed, though, I was emotionally wrung. *Why can't I be normal?* The question had been echoing in my mind for months. Remembering events of the last few days, I began thinking back over my life. *Had anything ever been normal? Is anyone normal? Is anyone good?* Then the more urgent question that had plagued me for years: *Will I ever feel safe?*

Stop whining, I ordered myself. *You just need sleep . . . or more drugs.*

Max interrupted my thoughts with curses. He had broken an expensive gold chain he always wore around his neck. He put it into the satchel for safekeeping. I collected the baggage, too tired to realize that Max was once again using me to distance himself from the possible consequences of his crimes. He went to get the car.

We put the costly suitcase in the trunk of his Mercedes. The ride home was grim. We were both burned out. Max took me to my place, a crash pad used by a variety of street people. For the past ten years, ever since I left home at age thirteen, I had seldom had any personal space. My friend, Robin, her ex-husband, and her teenage brother were there. Max provided us all with a supply of cocaine from the satchel, and Robin's brother left shortly after. We all did a couple lines, then went to bed. Max took off with the big money for Newport Beach.

"Where did you put the satchel?" Max's harsh voice dragged me rudely from oblivion. He had returned, extremely annoyed. It was late morning and the others had left.

"What?" I choked, uncomprehendingly. "What do you mean?"

"There was $19,000, some cocaine, and my gold chain in the satchel. What did you do with it? I was halfway to Newport when I saw it was missing. "

"I've no idea where it went. I didn't touch it."

"Don't lie to me. It was here last night."

I stumbled from the sagging bed, my eyes straining to focus. Ragged blankets and odd articles of clothing lay rumpled in the dingy room. I squinted around at my apartment. The dank odor of musty carpet filled the air. Max, unshaven and frazzled, kicked a dirty towel at his feet. A cockroach scuttled under the bed.

"I'm telling you the truth. I haven't seen your stupid satchel."

"Did you steal it?"

"Why would I do that?"

Max started pawing through my suitcase. Wadded clothes and stinking socks flew.

"Quit it. Cut it out."

"What's this?" He demanded. "My gold chain's in your suit-case."

My mind reeled. What was it doing there? I knew I hadn't put it there. Max spun around, his bloodshot eyes rotting cavities of rage.

"Where did you stash the money?"

"I . . . I didn't take it."

His sudden blow on my face slammed me to the floor.

"I don't care what you thought you could get away with, you whore, but you find my money and drugs. Hear me?"

I staggered to my feet, pleading. "Listen. I really didn't touch it. It wasn't me."

Max pulled a small handgun from his suitcase.

"It must have been one of the others."

He stared at me, his eyes narrowing.

"OK, baby. Now *you* listen. I don't care who did it. But you have a week to find out what happened to it or . . . " A steel point clicked cold below my ear. "I'll kill you."

CHAPTER

2

I slumped against the thin wall, my head spinning. *Here I am again. What did I do to deserve such a life?* I felt dirty. The trip to San Francisco had yanked my eyes open. The people I had known in the past ten years were considered small time, street people. Max was big time in comparison. Shouldn't I feel great? This was uptown living. So why did I feel like this? Why did I just want to die or get high? I made my way to the tiny bathroom, ignoring the vomit drying on the floor around the toilet and drew myself a hot bath. It didn't help.

The phone rang, interrupting my brooding.

"Cheri, thank God! We thought you were dead. Where've you been? Have you seen your car yet?" It was John, the club owner. His voice was hysterical.

"Slow down. My car? What about my car?" I had just bought a used Grand Prix with some extra cash I had earned prior to going to San Francisco. I had left it at the club for safekeeping.

"Someone smashed all the glass out of it. All the glass, head-lights, taillights, windshield, back window, side panels, even the glass in the dash control panel is shattered."

"What?" My mouth gaped.

"They also slit all the tires and rammed the passenger door with their car."

"I don't understand."

"Now the police want to question you."

The police? "Why?" Fear pummeled me again.

"They just want to be sure that you're alive. Whoever thrashed your car must have been really mad."

"But what have I done?"

"I da know. Hey, I'll send someone to pick you up. You're scheduled to work tonight." He hung up.

You're scheduled to work tonight. I knew John well. So that was the real reason for the call—my work.

I'm tired. Does anyone care? I am tired!

I had worked for John off and on for years, in fact since I was thirteen, when I first ended up on the streets. I supported myself and those who took me under their wings, or into their closets, by working in bars when I could get ID saying I was of age. Usually the club owners would get me the ID because their customers especially like to watch young girls dance—the younger the better. I felt angry about that right then. I felt angry about everything right then.

I dressed for work, smoked pot, did "crosstops," a form of speed, and waited for my ride. I always went to work high. When we pulled into the parking lot, I saw my car. I could not believe my eyes! It was much worse than I had imagined. Terror ripped into me. *Who did this? Why are they so angry with me?* I could still feel their rage. Long, deep gouges striped the side and top of the car. I did not even want to deal with it. I went inside the club, had a few shots of tequila, and went to work. The police didn't believe me when I said I had no idea who had done this. I really had no idea. That was the most terrifying. Whoever did this was obviously way out of control and clearly wanted to scare me. But why? I couldn't imagine, and gulping, I forced myself to forget it. Some of the girls were going to a party after work and invited me. I went. I dreaded going back to the apartment that night.

Everyone wants me dead, I thought, *including me. Why should I fear them? Maybe I should solve their problem.* The thought of suicide was my only peace. I already felt dead inside. Could anything more go wrong? Who had stolen the money? Who was trying to scare me?

Late the next morning, I had the mangled car towed to the shop. I needed someone to talk to, someone to listen. I decided to drop by home. I was desperate.

"Mom?" I rapped at the dilapidated screen door of my mom's house. The white paint was peeling, revealing drab brown beneath it. The front steps sagged, and newspapers were stacked on the porch, yellowing with age. A brown plot of dirt, never landscaped, graced the front as a yard. The windowpanes were yellowed slabs, caked with dust. I knocked louder, then let myself in. "Mom, are you home?"

"Cheri?" My mom, a middle-aged woman with graying brown hair, sat in the sparse living room watching TV. She stared at me, startled, like she'd seen a ghost, but she didn't get up. A weak smile struggled at one corner of her mouth.

"It's about time you showed up." Her voice was flat.

"Well, look who's here." My mom's boyfriend, my "stepfather" was sprawled on an old couch across the room. He looked up briefly and then back at the screen. "It's been a couple of years at least since we've seen you! It's good to know you're still alive."

"Yes, well, I . . . uh, just wanted to stop by and catch up," I said. My mother squirmed uncomfortably in her chair, rubbing her neck. "I just bought a new car."

"How nice." She looked like she was sitting on pins.

"Oh, it was vandalized the other night when I was in San Francisco."

"How awful. How was San Francisco?"

"Great. Still beautiful as ever."

"So, how is everything?" She shifted nervously and got up.

"Good." Mom was acting more ill at ease than usual.

She got out of her chair and walked over to her desk, looking among her stacks of papers. "I'm taking a psychology class. I've been working on a degree in social work."

I did a doubletake. "Social work, eh? What kind?"

"I'd like to work with children . . . uh, abused kids especially." She shuffled more papers.

"How neat!" I could have thrown up. I was feeling so desperate and alone. I wanted more than anything for my mom to love me. Now she was being trained to love others.

She turned to me, a thick envelope in hand. "I have something for you. I'd like you to read this. But not here, not now. When you get home." I took it, feeling some strange importance in it. I had never seen her like this. What could it be? She immediately started chatting with me. We were all smiles. My mind was all numb.

"I'm proud that you have never asked us for money or anything. I've always admired that about you." My "stepfather's" words shattered my charade. How dare he? I had been on the streets for the last ten years without any support or concern from them, yet when I did stop by to see them, I'd lie: "Everything is great."

What would he say if I told him I was dying inside? I was tired. I needed someone to hold me—to love me.

I bit my tongue. "Good to see you. Got to go." Abruptly, I headed for the door. Outside, my rage blinded me in tears. *Is anybody good?*

"My brother, Skip, stole the money," said Robin, my friend, a few days later. "He came back after we were asleep to steal cocaine from Max. He stole the satchel, but when he found the

$19,000, he put the chain in your suitcase to set you up. Would you believe he's already spent the money? He paid off his car, bought electronic equipment, and some furniture for his apartment.

"How did you figure it out?" I asked, relieved.

"I looked over his gate in the backyard and saw stacks of empty furniture, stereo, VCR, and other boxes. Come on. Where else would he get that kind of money?"

"Could you get him to admit it?"

"Nope. I even told him that Max threatened to kill me and my kids if I didn't get the money."

"So what did you do?"

"I just told Max and gave him Skip's address. He'll be working for Max until he's paid up, unless he'd rather die."

A thin tide of relief washed over me. But the feeling was empty. So I wasn't going to be murdered. Did it matter? I laughed at the irony. Now I really did want to die.

The auto body shop called to tell me that my car was ready. They had replaced all the glass, smoothed the dents, and touched up the paint. You couldn't tell it had ever been damaged. Then I noticed that the window on the passenger side had not been replaced.

"We don't believe that the door, before the accident, ever opened. Until you prove that the door opened, we cannot finish replacing the window," the insurance adjuster said. "Bring the glass back when you have proof that the door had opened, and we will be happy to put it in for you." He handed me the glass. No amount of arguing could change his mind. I left, disgusted.

I worked until 2:00 a.m. The night was long. While I was away in San Francisco, one of the girls I worked with had attempted suicide. I thought about her off and on for most of the night. I wondered what she had done to herself. Why had she failed?

A MIRACLE FROM THE STREETS

A tall, sandy-haired customer sat nearby at the counter where I rested for break. He watched me. Clean-cut and handsome, he was sipping orange juice. Odd, he wasn't smoking. His eyes drew me in. Annoyed, I averted my glance.

"My name's Jake."

"Uh-huh." I turned away. I'd had enough of these men.

"I'm not trying to hit on you. I just noticed you're upset. Could I treat you to dinner tomorrow?"

"I don't date customers." Tired, I took a drag of a fresh cigarette.

"Hey, you just look like you need a friend. You don't look happy here. Can I buy you a drink?"

I briefly stared at him, then his juice. "No thanks."

Now it was my shift to dance again, so I stood up. What was he doing in a place like this? Drinking orange juice? I didn't care to guess. I wasn't fooled.

"Here's my number if you ever need anything." His eyes were sympathetic. What did he care? I knew better. "I'll help if I can." He jotted his number down quickly and gave it to me before I could protest.

"Yeah, thanks." I was used to this. I put my mind on off and headed for the stage.

When I finished the shift, a cold, pouring rain drenched me on my way to the car. The rain blew bitterly in through the window.

While I was in the right-hand turn lane, waiting for the light to change, a car driving alongside swerved and plowed into me. Stunned, I screamed in fury and burst into tears. They squealed away. The rain was so heavy I couldn't even see what kind of car had hit me. My seat dripped with water, my face with tears. What could I do? My whole life was the scene of an accident. After checking on the damage, I drove on to my apartment, clenching the steering wheel, barely seeing the road through blurring eyes. Every time I turned the wheel, a scraping sound grated in my ears. All this work for nothing. My life was nothing as well.

It was 3:00 a.m. when I parked in front of my apartment. Walking up the dark corridor, I heard blaring music down the hall and saw rainbow-colored light bleeding under my door. In the front room, a naked man, a stranger, pranced on my rickety sofa, strumming the air wildly, pretending to play a guitar. His unfocused eyes saw me, and he grinned with grimy teeth. "Get out!" The music buried my rage.

"Just playing my air guitar," he babbled. He was tripping hard on LSD.

I started to cry again. I had to find a safe, quiet place. But where could I go? Almost everyone I knew was either on the streets or had the same kind of living arrangements as I had. And I certainly couldn't run to Max for protection. *Oh, God, I need help. What more can happen? Why do I even bother to go on living?*

CHAPTER 3

A gun would be quick, but I had none. Restless, I dumped the contents of my bedside drawer on the carpet, spilling bottles, syringes, and pills. *What am I searching for?* Drugs? I kicked through the mess. Not enough for an overdose. The morning was gray, as bleak and smoggy as my desperation. My thoughts were a foul bag smothering me. A thick white envelope stuck out from the pile, my mom's handwriting scrawled on the front. It remained unread. Picking it up, I ripped it open. What did she have to tell me that she couldn't say to my face? Hadn't she said enough? It wasn't a letter. It was a paper written for her psychology class for social work.

I hate you! I was just about to tear the paper up, but a line in red ink lunged at me.

"Please give this to Cheri."

I froze. Her instructor, Dr. Cabeen, wanted me to read this paper. Why? The decaying hands of fear, so familiar, groped for me. Did she confess her hatred of me? Did she write about how I ruined her life? What a horrible child I was? I always knew she didn't like me, that she was bitter at my birth. If she never heard from me again, it would be fine. Did I want to make my suspicions reality? I winced, my breath cut short.

My mom wrote about her early childhood in Canada. She was emotionally and sexually abused. Her mother left her with an aunt for many years. Later, her mother got married, picked up my mom, and moved to California. My mom had never told me anything about her childhood. I shivered. It almost seemed as if I were staring in a mirror, reading my own story. When she wrote about her sadness, my eyes misted. I wanted to hold her, to tell her I was sorry. Her pain was mine.

She met my father and quickly became pregnant. She was fourteen, he, sixteen. They lived a fairy-tale happiness, one they thought would never end. Though their parents disapproved, they let them marry and helped them financially. My parents were overjoyed when their first child, Debbie, my older sister, was born. I started to cry. *Why couldn't I be Debbie?*

Debbie was only two months old when my mom found herself pregnant again. A deep depression settled on her. Everything changed. My dad started to drink more. My parents began to argue. When my dad got needy, it disgusted her, and she withdrew from him. From everyone. She wrote about her desperation. She attempted to self abort by taking hot baths, pills, and by even using coat hangers, but without success. In spite of her best efforts, I was born . . . into this mess.

Reading, I cried. I remembered even as a small child trying to get my mom to like me. I knew she hated me, but I didn't know why. I would sit around and scheme up ways to get her to laugh. I believed if I could make myself smarter, cuter, or funnier, she would love me. Yet everything I tried only made her angrier. At age three I would sit in front of the TV with the family, everyone watching but me. I was silently rehearsing how to be funnier, how to be different so she . . . so they would love me. It never worked. It still has not worked.

My father was only mentioned to explain his drinking and physical abuse of her. Did she know that all my early memories of him were of him touching me sexually? I remember only little, and what I do is not good. I would only see him on an occasional Christmas or birthday. He would take me and my sister and brother for a visit to his warehouse where he worked, molest us, and drop us at home. How often I wished he was normal and that he loved me, but then he would hurt me again. I felt so dirty. *Is this love?* I wondered each time, then shut my eyes.

"I hated her," I read. It was true. My heart plunged. Her words, tied on like rocks, sunk me in the muck of rejection. The "her" was me. I had lied to myself, trying to believe it wasn't me. If it wasn't for my sister, she would love me. If it wasn't for her working late nights, she would love me. If it wasn't for my dad beating her, if I could be funnier, if I was prettier . . . It didn't matter. She still hated me. My parents had considered giving me up for adoption. They had lined up a couple but changed their mind at the last minute. My grandmother convinced them that keeping me was the right thing.

When I was born, my mom hated feeding me. She sat outside my bedroom door crying, as I wailed inside the room. She feared to come inside for what she might do to me. She'd throw me to my father to take care of.

Now, surrounded by my drug paraphernalia, my empty drawer, my broken life, I sobbed. A picture of an ugly baby, drool running down her face, filled my mind. Me. As a family joke, my mom and sisters teased me by threatening to show it to a boyfriend. "This is what your kids will look like," they'd say. I understood why this child . . . why I . . . looked so pathetic, so uncared for.

In amazement, I read about her guilt. She felt responsible for the fact that I had been on the streets since age thirteen, a drug addict. In depression and anger she had rejected me. Our family was set up to reject this second child. There was, and is, nothing I could have done to get acceptance or love from my family. I dropped the paper, stunned. At last the truth. For the first time in my life.

"This was never about you." It was almost as if a voice spoke to me.

I turned, glancing at wisps of sunlight streaming through a high window. I was alone. *What? It was never about me? So I just happened to be born into a mess with two kids pretending to be parents, trying to play grownup? Never about me?*

The unbreakable ropes with the rocks holding me under snapped. A dizzy lightness swept me. *Never about me?* A new feeling tugged me, towing me upward away from my muddy pain, leaving a stream like bubbles and light and hope. I never had felt it before. *Never about me! Maybe I'm not such a bad person.*

Maybe I am OK.

"I love you."

"What?" I cried out loud. The light made patches on the floor. I sprang to my feet, letting the paper fall, crunching on syringes and bottles. "Who are you? Where?"

Silence.

A peaceful silence, warm. I was loved. "What does this mean? What do I do?"

I sank back down, watching the strands of light as they stretched across the floor. Time slid by.

I have to get out of here. Restlessness seized me. By now the afternoon shadows deepened and I needed to find a quiet place where no one would intrude, where no one got high, a place to think and sleep. I had to escape from this dark, junkie apartment. But where? With whom? I didn't know anyone who didn't do drugs.

Then I remembered. Jake.

CHAPTER

4

hy don't we spend some time at my sister's in Placerville for a while," Jake asked one day. It was a week since I had moved in with him. I had never tried to clean up before, and I never imagined it would be this hard. While Jake was straight, not into drugs, his help still had a price. We quickly became sexually involved, which for me was always the cost. Yet this orange-juice guy seemed different. Would he stick around?

"It's a lovely place in the mountains. The perfect place for you to rest."

"Wow! I could really use the retreat," I said, thinking a backwoods haven in the California mountains would be close to heaven, whatever that was. I've always lived in the city. It was the only thing I knew.

"One thing, though," Jake added. "My sister's a very conservative Christian."

"What does that mean?"

"Well, my whole family actually is pretty straight. Nobody

smokes, drinks, or anything. It'll be a different speed for you, that's for sure." He chuckled.

"Great. Just what I need. Someone lecturing me on the dangers of smoking or handing me a pamphlet about God." While I hadn't taken any hard drugs for a few days, I was smoking cigarettes by the packful.

"Come on. They're nice folk. Trust me. You'll really like them."

Trust? Whatever! I bit my lip. *Trust?* Even though I had sensed God while reading my mom's autobiography, I didn't associate Him with Christians. Christians were people, and I had a hard time trusting people. I just needed a quiet place to heal, whatever that meant. *And don't talk to me about trust.*

On the curvy mountain roads to Placerville, Jake chattered all about his family. As he described them, wonderful and perfect, an anger seethed inside. Why was I so angry? *How will I act in front of his family? In front of normal people? In front of normal people and me without drugs?* The more he talked, the more I panicked. *Man! I wish I would have brought some drugs. I don't care if I'm trying to kick them. Just a little bit of something. Anything.*

We arrived at the large log cabin nestled in the pine-covered foothills of the Sierras as the sun sank behind the hills behind us. Light gleamed from the large windows, shining out on the landscaped lawn. Our car crunched up the graveled driveway, rolling next to one of the many cars parked there. I shrank just looking at the size of the house.

"Can we walk around a little bit before we go in?" I asked Jake. My palms were rivers.

"No, come on. It'll be OK."

"They are not going to like me."

"Yes they will. You'll be fine." Jake guided me to the door.

I frantically dug out one of the many psychological masks I wore. It screamed, "I am fine, and if you don't like it, so what. I don't care." Without a mask I was lost, because I had no idea who I was without one. Reality sped faster than I had inner legs to outrun it. No drugs now to rely on, to hide behind. *Who am I? How do I act? Get me out of here!*

Jake introduced me to his sister Donna and her husband, Don. Donna was a petite middle-aged woman with short, brown, wavy hair and silver wisps, a dimpled chin, and discerning eyes. Her smile beamed from a youthful face, though wrinkled, clean without makeup. She looked toned and fit, a bundle of energy. She welcomed and hugged me before I could shrink. I smelled a whiff of homemade bread. When Jake introduced me to his four neices, their husbands, and all their children, I couldn't keep up with all the names. Like falling deep in a good dream, I sank back in a soft sofa and watched them laughing, catching up. They were all so friendly and beautiful. Jake hadn't seen them in a while. They tried to draw me out. The cozy living room wafted with warm bread smells from the kitchen. Their rising, falling voices hypnotized me. While the children frolicked in the hallways and bedrooms, I watched the scene tranced, re-moved, a screen of detached distance between them and me, me and perfection. I was an outsider. It wasn't what anyone did, I just had no experience being real or laughing with someone I love. In their smiles and their tones and their eyes, they loved each other. I watched in amazed silence.

"What's the topic of the study tonight?" someone asked, pulling out a Bible.

I tensed.

"Justification by faith," Donna said. "My Australian friend, Michael, will be coming over to lead out." The doorbell rang.

"So they've met here to study the Bible?" I whispered to Jake, remembering his warning. "Yes. They meet together every Friday night to study and spend time together. I'm going to the kitchen to talk with my neice Julie. If you want, you can come."

"Thanks." *Every Friday? How nice.* I wasn't too sure about this Bible thing, but if it took the focus off me . . . I'd listen awhile.

Michael talked long on the "sin problem."

Oh, great. I sank further in my seat. *I could enlighten you a bit on the subject.* I wanted to hide because they spoke of the sin problem as if it was "out there," someone else's problem.

The sin problem's right here. You're looking at her.

On they philosophized. I felt sick and hopeless. How could I share the things I was dealing with or trying to change? *What am I doing here? Who am I trying to kid?* I pushed up from my spot in the earnest discussion and went outside to smoke.

The night sky was a twinkling mass of dot-to-dots, tiny and unnumbered. I tried to connect them. *Who am I, trying to make sense of my place anyway? I'm but a speck, alone and misplaced in the universe.*

"God, are you really there?" The light from the house streamed out onto the lawn, casting long shadows to the pines at the forest's edge. "Can you see me?" The night wind blew softly.

I opened the door and quietly came back in.

"I felt guilty buying a dress because I could have given the money to someone in need," I heard one of Jake's neices say. "Or I should have spent the time cheering someone up at a nursing home."

Just great. I stared at the carpet, my hopelessness growing. Someone was watching me. I glanced up and caught Donna's eyes. *What does she think about me in her house? What did Jake tell her about me?* I looked away.

"When I listen to a secular radio station, I feel guilty," another added. "But sometimes I just like the music." Words like vanity, tithe, jewelry, and church attendance popped up. I continued staring at the carpet. I could never share any of my reality with these people. Never.

" 'For God so loved the world, that he gave his only begotten Son, that whosoever believeth in him should not perish, but have everlasting life.' John 3:16," Michael read.

What's your point?

"We're all sinners. We've all fallen short of the glory of God."

*If only you knew, buddy. What would you say to **me**?* He continued.

"Remember the adulterous woman, Mary, who was brought to Jesus?"

The only Mary I've heard about was supposed to be Jesus' mother. What are you talking about? My embarrassment kept me from asking. *They'll want to know why I'm so interested.*

"Jesus didn't judge her. He forgave her, in fact. It didn't matter what she had done. He accepted and loved her anyway."

How nice. This makes me sick. I excused myself and went back outside to smoke.

I want to go home. I don't fit in here.

That's a laugh. I don't fit in anywhere. I went upstairs to bed. Going through drug withdrawal made my moods swing crazily.

"Can you grab me something sweet?" I asked Jake before I went to sleep. "Some chocolate or soda would be great."

"Donna is a vegetarian; she doesn't eat sugar, and there's not a caffeinated drink in the house."

"What? Whoa, now I'm going through withdrawal from caffeine, sugar, and chocolate too. I guess I am going to clean up, whether I like it or not." I fell into a restless sleep.

Warm sun played on my bed when I woke up. I heard conversation in the other room, and rolling over, I lay there listening. Their comfortable chatter amazed me. Something was different, but I couldn't pin it down. That was it! The humor and language was pleasant. Funny, no swearing, no put-downs, and no sarcasm—no little slams. Entranced, I could have listened all day, but suddenly I looked at the clock—2:45 p.m.! *Oh no! How can I face them now? Good morning. Yes. I am a lazy bum—unlike you.*

No one seemed to mind. When I joined them, they tried to draw me into their conversation. We listened to music together, and then they took me on a hike through the foothills. An invisible wall, hard and cruel, still blocked me off from them. My experiences were so different and ugly that I would never have a *nice* life, a *nice* conversation that is real.

As darkness poked through the pines, many left, but some stayed for a game of Uno in the kitchen.

"Come play with us, Cheri."

"No, thanks. I'm rather tired. Maybe later." *What is Uno?* I couldn't play any game without being high on drugs. I escaped to the quiet living room. In the dim light, I settled on the cozy sofa, curled my legs up, and gazed out the vaulted window at the dark. The stereo softly played a Sandi Patti tape. Her voice lilted, soared, and soothed. Tears wet my eyes and slid down my cheeks. In the darkness I didn't brush them away.

Donna came in and sat beside me, not speaking. We listened silently for a long time. "What did you think about Michael's study on justification by faith," she asked at last.

"I don't know." I didn't look at her.

She talked softly about her experience with Jesus and His love. I listened for a long time. "God knows us. He knows our condition," she said. My ears perked up. "More importantly, even the very best of us are full of sin. No sin is worse than another."

"What?" I lashed out, half rising. "You're wrong. You have no clue what you're talking about. I'm not stupid enough to believe that all sins are the same. That God looks at me in the same way He looks at . . . at . . . you . . . these people." I swept my hand off in a vague direction. Startling myself, I sank back and took a deep breath. *Calm down!* But I couldn't.

"I want to believe you, sure, but it's just talk, nice talk. It doesn't work for me." *Hand me a pamphlet and go back to your family.* I raged. Donna said nothing.

"I need to smoke."

"I'm going to the bathroom," she said.

When I returned, Donna was listening to another tape.

"Amazing grace! how sweet the sound That saved a wretch like me!" it sang.

Oh, brother. "You talk easily of forgiveness and love," I blurted. My cigarette had not calmed me. "But I have never seen that in my life. Everyone has his own motives." To help others in an honest, altruistic way is something I'd never witnessed. I didn't believe I was seeing it now from her.

"God is a compassionate, loving Father who longs for us, His children, to come home to Him. But we were stuck in our mess. Jesus, God's son, died for us, to bring us back to God."

I listened politely, my teeth clenched. "If once we ask God for forgiveness, He forgives completely. He erases and forgets our sins. We become new . . ."

My mind screeched over and over. *You don't know the things I've done. If you knew me, really knew me, you'd not even talk to me; you'd kick me out of your home.* She continued, but I barely heard her. Anger squirted black through my veins. She wasn't a bad person, no; but how dare she rattle on to me of love! My life and death were at stake, and sitting next to me was this naive woman speaking casually about love. I would prove her a fake. She would see, she would know, and she would have nothing to say.

"I need a cigarette."

"I need to use the bathroom."

CHAPTER

5

"Tell me about your past, your family," Donna said. "What brought you to this point in life?"

I hesitated. *Well, she asked for it. But where to start?*

"My mom tried to self-abort me six different times."

"Six?"

"She used coat hangers, causing only hemorrhage, not miscarriage."

She started to speak, but I interrupted.

"The only father I've ever known was an alcoholic who sexually abused me. So when you talk about God as my Father, I can't grasp that picture. My family tolerates me, but they do not love me. They never have.

"I spent most of my childhood trying to get my mom to love me, most of my life, rather. I'd blame others for her feelings toward me. If not for my dad or her children, she would've loved me. If not for my sister, if not for the lack of money . . .

"When I was three, I remember, huddled in my room upstairs, listening to my mom and dad screaming. Trying to ignore the fighting, I began to sing while I played with my doll. Soon I was covering my ears. I couldn't concentrate and hid my head under my pillow, so afraid.

I heard a loud thud and the screaming stopped. I couldn't breathe. Even though I knew I'd get in trouble for going downstairs, I had to risk it. Mom was in trouble. I ran into the living room toward her. When she turned, all I saw was blood, dark red blood, running through her fingers. I froze. She held her hands up to her face trying to stop the blood from dripping onto the carpet. She pushed by me, heading for the bathroom. I wanted to help her, but I didn't know what to do.

"Get into your room now!" she yelled. Helpless, I sat in my room for hours, clutching my baby doll, listening to them fight. Then my dad left to drink.

"Sometimes he'd take us kids with him. He left us in the car, sometimes for hours. My grandmother would sometimes find us in the car sitting in the parking lot of his favorite bar. She'd yell at him and take us home. My grandparents were angry at Dad for being a poor father and sorry for Mom that she had to deal with these things. But nobody seemed to care that we had sat for hours in urine, locked in a cold car. They'd clean us up, send us to our room so they could talk, but no one looked at us. No one held me. I learned by four not to think about what was happening, whether it was fair or not or how I felt. I learned I didn't matter."

I stopped talking, self-consciousness stifling me. *Maybe she thinks I'm just feeling sorry for myself. It does sound like I'm whining.* But a weight finally lifted just saying this stuff out loud to somebody. I looked at Donna, she at me.

"I need to smoke."

"I need to go to the bathroom."

When I came back to the living room, Donna was gone.

Do you blame her? I asked myself. *Do you think anyone really cares about your problems? Who wants to listen to you cry about your life?* My sadness twisted into anger.

She's giving me lip service. The love she believes in is a lie. I proved her a phony, and it didn't take as long as I expected. I went out for a short walk and another cigarette.

The cabin door opened behind me.

"I was wondering where you went," Donna said. "I love looking at these mountains. I often take night walks beneath this starry sky. I feel so small in the universe when I look up."

"Yeah. I'm used to smog and street lights."

We sat quietly together on the grass looking up. Could she sense that I did not know how to just sit and talk? The pine needles whispered, and the crickets chirped. Though uncomfortable, I couldn't remember feeling so safe and so at peace.

"How is your relationship with your parents now?"

"I haven't seen my dad for a long time. He left my mom when I was four. He was just gone one day when we got home. I only saw him a couple times afterward while growing up. When I was seven, his visits stopped. I searched for him when I was twelve. I had blocked all memories of the abuse and had built my dad up in my mind. If I found him, he would love me. After all, he was my father. I needed someone to love me. To tell me I was OK.

"Why hasn't he visited me? I thought. He lived only fifteen miles from me. I had a hard time keeping the hero image that I fantasized alive. Finally I went to find him.

"I looked twice at the address on the napkin. This can't be my dad's house! Staring at the dingy tan buildings that looked more like cardboard boxes than apartments, my fantasy began to crumble. I'd always imagined that my dad had a big house with a manicured lawn. A house that did not have brown grass and weeds like my house. But this was worse. It had *no* grass. It was a rundown flat in Long Beach, surrounded by asphalt. The building was shaped like a horseshoe with a center court crammed with junky cars. Dingy miniblinds, closed tight, covered the small window on apartment 5. I almost turned to leave.

"Come on! Knock on the door! I commanded myself. I can't! And what if he really doesn't want to see me? Desperation forced me. I knocked.

" 'Why, look who's here!' His face brightened. Rather thin and dark, he wore a grimy workshirt, opened wide at the collar. 'Come in.' I sighed, relieved.

" 'Why haven't you ever come to see me?' I asked him.

" 'I didn't think you missed me.' *Yeah, right.* All his excuses for not visiting me through the years were weak. He knew it. We dropped the subject and babbled about what we were doing in our lives now. His apartment was small, more like a tiny motel room. We went out to eat, and he took me shopping. 'You can spend the night, so you'll need some pajamas,' he told me. He bought me a cute lacy teddy. My eyes grew large—it was the most beautiful gift I'd ever received.

" 'Why don't you put it on,' he asked me when I got home. I didn't think anything wrong with his request, so I changed, but then I realized it was small and see through.

" 'I feel uncomfortable coming out in this,' I said from the bathroom.

" 'That's ridiculous. I'm your father,' " he assured. 'Let's see how you look.' I came out.

"It was late, so my dad brought out a cot for me, and I went to sleep. I woke up scared, smelling alcohol, hearing heavy breathing, and . . . I desperately pretended to be asleep. Then I went blank. The next day I got up, acted like nothing had happened, and then ran. Why couldn't my father just be normal? Why couldn't he love me?"

I paused in my story, sick. I had never told anyone about my dad. Donna was silent, and I couldn't look at her. When I did, I saw sadness, not judgment.

I turned away, feeling ugly and dirty and . . .

I felt her hand on my shoulder. The mountain wind blew

chilly, rustling our hair, filling our silence.

"I really need a cigarette."

"Go ahead," Donna said.

"Well," I hedged, the familiar self-consciousness again.

"Go ahead. I'm going to the bathroom."

Getting cold, I wandered back to the house. Her family was still playing table games in the kitchen, laughing and hooting. In the living room again, I poked curiously through the books on the bookshelf.

"Here's a story I'd like to read you," Donna said, returning to find me. "Do you remember the story Michael mentioned about Mary?" She pulled out a book, *The Desire of Ages* from the shelf.

"Yeah, but I'm confused. I thought Mary was the mother of Jesus, not a prostitute."

"This is Mary Magdalene, a different woman. Here, let me read you the story." Opening the book, she read about Jesus having dinner at a man named Simon's house. In came Mary, a woman of questionable character, a prostitute. Forgiven by Jesus, she threw herself at his feet, washing them with her tears. Mary, in complete abandon, poured perfume over Jesus' head to anoint Him (whatever that meant). Oblivious to others, the only thing she cared about was Jesus. He had given her back her life, and she longed to express her love.

The presence I felt after I had read my mom's autobiography flashed through me. *Was it Jesus who had spoken? Was it His voice I had heard? Had He forgiven me too?*

"I know what . . ." I was going to tell Donna about the experience, but I stopped.

"What?" Donna asked.

I shook my head. "Nothing." Protective, I didn't want anyone to take it away from me. Someone would say it was all in my head. *Never*, I cried. It was too precious to be ripped away.

CHAPTER

6

D id you feel loved by anyone growing up? What about your grandparents?" Donna's voice wavered, sadly. Her eyes touched me, brimming with sympathy and sadness. Was it for me? I never let myself grasp the full impact of my childhood or my life. It overwhelmed me. It was easier to stay uninvolved, uncaring, detached from myself.

"It's OK to be sad for that child, for yourself," her eyes said. Was Jesus sad for me too? "So tell me about your grandparents." she repeated. I sighed.

"They never hid their hatred of me. While my mom was pregnant with me, my grandma was pregnant with her third child. While my grandma's pregnancy had no complications, her baby, Patrick, was born with severe birth defects. He was a hemophiliac, had a double cleft palate, and physical deformities. Overwhelmed with his medical problems, their sadness turned to anger. Then I, unlike their baby, was born healthy, unwanted. The anger grew. It was unfair."

Donna clicked her tongue and shook her head.

"On the way to a doctor's appointment, Patrick, five, complained he was sick to his stomach. "Don't throw up in the car," she threatened. "Wait 'til I pull over." Patrick couldn't. Scared to let her know, he inhaled the vomit and suffocated. Somehow, they blamed his death on me."

"What?" Donna stood up from her chair, indignant. "What did you have to do with it?"

"I don't know. I was still alive, healthy, and unwanted. Well, they never forgave me for Patrick's death. I didn't have a clue of the emotional issues involved. The anger, now guilt, my grandma felt because of her part in her son's death turned hot toward me. My grandpa ignored me. I felt nothing from him. I am not sure which was worse."

Donna sat down again, her forehead wrinkled in attentiveness.

"I'd watch my grandparents play and laugh with my sisters and brother, but with me it was either cold teasing or sarcasm. My grandma's barbed humor was cruel. When she'd make me cry, she'd laugh. She'd laugh it off if I told anyone. "You know I was only playing.""

"Wasn't there anyone who cared about you?" Donna asked. "Someone who did make a difference? Surely someone?"

"Yeah, one. My Auntie Kay, my grandma's sister. She was an actress and so funny. I usually only saw her at Christmas. Whenever I'd see her, I'd run and leap into her arms. 'How's my little Cheri?' she'd squeal. She always seemed glad to see me."

My voice grew animated. "She'd start our visits with a joke. It was always the same joke, but we loved it."

"What was it," Donna asked. "Do you remember?"

"Yes. After everything I say, you say pea soup. OK?"

Donna smiled. "OK."

"What did you have for breakfast?"

"Pea soup."

"What did you have for lunch?"

"Pea soup."

"What did you have for dinner?"

"Pea soup."

"What did you do all night?"

"Pea soup," Donna laughed.

"We'd collapse in giggles. She'd always told adventure stories of the theater. Her son George was also in show business. He had small parts in the *Little Rascals* when he was small. I even saw a newspaper clipping of George being held by the famous actress Mae West. Mae West had said he was a talented actor. I could listen to my aunt for hours.

"On my eighth Christmas, I jumped out of the car at my grandma's house so excited to see her. She was the real reason for my joy. Christmas and presents were nice, but they didn't hold me or make me laugh. I couldn't wait to hear our joke.

" 'Is Auntie Kay here yet?' I yelled to my mom, bounding with anticipation.

" 'Come over here and be quiet,' my mom commanded. I ran to her, still jumping.

" 'Your Auntie Kay is dead. Don't say anything, because you'll upset your grandma.'

"Dead? I felt clubbed in the stomach. 'No! No! No!' I couldn't breathe. My face contorted into tears and disbelief.

" 'Stay outside 'til you stop crying,' Mom said, leaving me stunned and sobbing.

"I walked over to the rocks around the garden and sat. Dead? What was death, anyway? I didn't understand, but I knew I'd never see my aunt again. My soul ripped inside out. Let me die too! Please. Oh, Auntie Kay! I sobbed for a long time. I tried to stop, but the more I tried, the more tears burst. I was drowning. 'Please don't leave me here, Auntie Kay,' I sniffled.

"The sky was a concrete gray of loneliness. Suddenly the clouds broke and a ray of sun peeked through.

" 'What did you have for breakfast?' I heard Auntie Kay's

echo in my head.

" 'Pea soup.'

"Somehow I knew it was going to be OK. We'd see each other again someday."

Never before had I told anyone how much I missed my aunt or how special she was to me. Nobody had cared before. My self-consciousness revived.

What am I doing telling this anyway? I don't even know you, Donna. Yet I was amazed at how easy it was to talk to her.

"Was God there with me on the rocks that day as a child?" I looked out the window at the darkness. It was getting late. I poked at the carpet. "Do you think God used the sun peeking through the clouds to comfort me?"

I glanced up. Donna was crying.

No one had ever cried for me. *Why did she care?*

CHAPTER 7

"If you'd rather not talk about all this, I'd understand," Donna said, coming into the sunny living room after breakfast the next morning. "I hurt just listening to you tell about it. I cannot imagine how you must feel." She stood by the window, gazing out at the pine cone and green-needled morning.

I studied her a long time, baffled by the sincerity in her eyes. I had spent half the night dumping myself on her. *Why does she care? Why is she being so wonderful to me? What's her real motive?*

"It feels good to talk to someone about all this. I have a bad habit of talking too much." *That's not the only bad habit I have. I wonder if she knows how messed up I am? What did Jake tell her?* A sliver of fear pricked me.

"What happened after your Auntie Kay died?" Donna plopped near me in an easy chair, turning all her attention on me. Her interest was more than politeness, for I knew she had better things to do. *Well, she hasn't heard the half of it yet.*

I closed my eyes. My memory lay like a city slum, grafitied and forgotten, thick with muddy smog. *What had happened?* The haze blurred my recall, because pain had blocked the memory out. *Can I stare at this again?*

"Soon after my aunt died, my leg and knee started killing me. Walking was torture. The occasional bursts of pain froze me, and I would just sit and cry. The pain soon throbbed constantly. Mom, annoyed more than usual, took me to get my leg evaluated at the Children's Hospital. An X-ray revealed a malformed right hip, and the doctors diagnosed me with a disease called Legg-Calvé-Perthes. Not only did I have to start therapy right away, but for the next couple of years I had to wear a leg brace and walk with crutches. While that freaked me, it turned out being the best thing I could have hoped for."

"Why is that?" Donna's forehead wrinkled, puzzled.

"The nurses and doctors were funny and seemed to like me. My mom spent more time with me. In the clinic she played a real mom, like she was concerned about me or something."

Donna frowned. "She pretended she loved you in front of the doctors?"

"It was great! And therapy meant coming down to the hospital three times a week to go swimming. There would be lots of other kids there to swim with. I was thrilled. Even the braces weren't so bad. They were weird at first, but suddenly they were cool. The hospital fascinated me. When people there talked to me, they really talked to me. They would look at me and even ask questions to make sure I understood what was being said.

" 'Let's stop at Denny's for breakfast,' Mom said when we went to therapy the first time. I couldn't believe it, Mom and me—going to breakfast? Usually we kids seldom ate with our parents. We ate in the kitchen by ourselves. This hip disease and pain were worth it!

"At the clinic, the nurse asked me to put on my bathing suit. Going to the doctor's for swimming? What fun! At the pool I was shocked to see kids there with serious deformities. One kid had only one arm, and one leg was skinny. I tried not to stare.

The nurse put us on a machine that swung around and lowered us into the pool. Soon we began to play with each other. The kid with no arm and the skinny leg beat me in a race across the pool. No way! He was a great swimmer. After a while, the deformed kids seemed the same to me as other kids. One by one, the physical therapist would check our 'range of motion.' 'Exercises will keep you strong,' she said. It hurt, especially when she twisted my leg out to the side. 'Got to stretch it in every way to keep it flexible,' she explained. The pain didn't matter, because I knew she was trying to help, and her touch felt good."

"So why did your leg brace and crutches help you?" Donna steered back to my statement.

"Special attention. I rented them out at school. The kids would pay me some of their lunch money to wear the brace and crutches. Some would have races with them. Life couldn't have been better."

Donna smiled. "Did home life get better?"

"At first, but not for long. My older sister hated the attention I was getting. That wasn't how it was supposed to be, in her opinion. She would pick fights and blame them on me. She'd leave a mess or break things and say I did it. By the time I was ten, we were fighting all the time. No matter what happened, it was my fault. I constantly heard about how good my older sister was, the little princess. No matter how I tried to do the right thing, to find ways to get my mom to love me, it was a hopeless cause."

"How can things get worse than that?" Donna asked, looking frustrated.

"Because the dream cracked, showing the corpse rotting behind the china doll paint.

'Why don't we send her away?' I overheard Mom and her boyfriend debate one night.

"What? Where?

"No, they wouldn't send me away. Would they?

"How could they?

"Why? I smothered the pillow tight over my head. I didn't hear it. It won't happen.

"Panic pushed me to change my behavior. I did what I was told. I didn't talk too much. I chewed my food carefully, because of the way my chewing sometimes annoyed Mom. 'You look like a cow,' she'd say. But the more I watched my behavior, the more chaotic my life became."

"You were an emotional mess," Donna empathized.

" 'We're sending you to Canada,' Mom announced one day. 'It's for your own good.'

"The scaled nightmare struck. My heart froze, unable to run. It was true? How could it be good?

" 'I lived with this aunt when I was little too. It will be wonderful for you.'

"I stared at her. I didn't say a word in protest. It wouldn't help. My lungs wheezed with heavy disbelief.

" 'You'll be going to Toronto. I think it's some 3,000 miles away.' She babbled on.

'It's for your good, as well as ours. We'll all be happier this way.'

"I'm not stupid, I cried inside. You'll forget me for sure. How am I going to get you to love me from Canada? The thought coiled and squeezed around me, crushing every hope in my body."

CHAPTER

8

Just like that I was sent away. No big deal. My family threw me out like yesterday's stinking garbage. If I had blamed my mom, the pain would have killed me, so I blamed everyone else. I felt boxed in an invisible cube, the sides as strong as iron, the air as thick as death. I could see and hear and touch and taste, but it wasn't real, it wasn't me. I didn't belong here. I didn't belong anywhere."

"Did your mom drive you to Canada?" Donna asked.

"No. She didn't want anything more to do with me. My grandparents drove. By dropping me off, they would get to visit with all the relatives. Grandma talked nonstop about how great it would be to see hers. Grandpa would see his. But I would stay, and Canada would be my home.

"That's not fair! I want to go home too. Please don't leave me there, I screamed as they planned and laughed and ignored me."

Donna sighed, her face gentle with listening.

"A big party waited for us at my Aunt Joyce's house. She's my

The Cheri Peters Story

grandmother's sister, but not the aunt I would stay with, Auntie Mae. My grandparents acted as if they loved me. Nice. But why? I met my cousins, Lori and Craig, and my Aunt Laura and Uncle Bob. Everyone was friendly and excited.

"The next day I met Auntie Mae, white-haired and wrinkled. She rushed at me and squeezed my breath away, but I just hung there, limp. Her house reeked of old-fashionedness and baby powder. Knickknacks, statues, and dolls lay everywhere, cluttering up the place. A picture of Jesus, His painted eyes empty, stared at me from the wall. I couldn't stay here! Grandma didn't want to stay there either. They chatted superficially for a while, then my grandparents left to visit another relative. I bolted after them.

" 'You're staying here,' Grandma's stern voice snapped, then slowly changed to a softer tone for the benefit of Auntie Mae. 'We'll be back in a little while.' My tears welled up, but Grandma's withering glance stopped them from erupting.

" 'OK.' You can't do this! . . . I hate you! . . . Please don't leave me. I couldn't say it.

" 'Are you hungry?' Auntie Mae squealed high as if she was speaking to a small child or a wounded animal. I nodded, sullen.

"Moving around the kitchen she reminisced about my mother and the years she spent 'here in this very house.' She loved my mom. 'Not a day goes by that I don't pray for her and you children.' While now her voice soothed me, I didn't let her know that I wanted her to keep talking. In fact, I deliberately scorned her stories. I answered shortly in one- or two-word replies, and when she pushed me to elaborate, sarcasm spoke. I just wanted to go home."

"Did your grandparents come back, as they promised?" Donna asked.

"Yes, they came back the next day brimming over about the great time they had had. There was a party at my great-uncle's house.

" 'Can I come this time?' I asked my grandparents. They said Yes.

" 'See you Monday,' Auntie Mae said. 'Have fun at the ranch.'

"We're staying the weekend at a ranch? With horses and cows and sheep? I'd never seen a ranch before, and excitement flooded me. When would we get there?

"The ranch ended up being a big, flat dirt lot. As we drove into the dusty driveway, people, my relatives, were running everywhere. I gaped at the huge eighteen-wheelers parked all around the property.

" 'Do you want to climb inside a Big Rig?' my great-uncle Alfie asked me.

" 'Cool!' I had never seen the inside of a semi before, and climbing into the trucks was fun. My cousin Lori (my age) showed up, so I felt like I knew someone now. People kept arriving. My grandfather's family kept getting bigger, louder, and crazier.

"Alfie opened kegs of beer and lighted the barbecue. His wife, eight months pregnant, gorged us with a never-ending array of snacks. The adults drank and drank, and the more they drank, the wilder they got.

"*BOOSH!* A water balloon exploded out of nowhere, soaking me as I played tag. No one was around. *SPLAT!* Another one. It came from the roof. Lori and I sped to find our own supply of balloons and began pelting them at innocents. Soon a full-scale balloon war left everyone soaking. Discovering how to climb to the roof, I sneaked up, hoisting a huge water balloon. Hearing the secret bomber, I tiptoed across the shingles toward the other side of the ridge. Rising above the ridge, I hurled my weapon. *SPLAT!* A perfect hit.

" 'Hey!' Alfie yelped. He was the secret bomber. He chased me down the ladder and around the yard. He caught me, gasping with laughter, wrestled me to the ground, and tickled me. Then he carried me, kicking madly, over to the green garden hose and drenched me.

" 'I really like you!' Alfie said, grinning. 'You're funny.' I blushed, the warmth spreading from my face inward. I liked him too."

Donna chuckled. "He sounds like he really made you feel special. How neat."

"That night everyone settled down in the living room and told stories about their childhood together and relatives dead or gone. I savored the 'normalness.' Maybe I could stay here instead of going to live with stuffy Aunt Mae.

"The night grew late, and we kids, who acted more grownup than the adults, were sent to bed. In a small den with a love seat and a mattress on the floor, Lori and I made our beds. The day still excited us, so we looked up at the dark, chattering about everything. I liked Lori. She talked about tobogganing, ice skating, and all her friends. I could join her, because I would be around. How exciting!

"Please don't ask me why I was sent here. I winced. She didn't. It was as if she already knew. Grateful, I was relieved not to talk about it. I lay there thinking about the day, the water balloons, my new friend, and Alfie's teasing. *He really likes me! Maybe Canada won't be so bad after all.*"

CHAPTER

9

It was late, and now the house was silent, dark. Suddenly, we heard a muffled clomp coming down the stairs. Both of us, hushed and tense, pretended to be sound asleep. The study door creaked open.

"A hairy hand clamped suddenly over my mouth, but I kept my eyelids clenched. My stomach lurched, and my heart skidded as another hand pulled my nightgown up over my hips. I wanted to scream, to kick, to run away, but fright paralyzed me. Kissed on the neck and pulled closer, I grew sicker. The reek of alcohol and cigarettes was so strong I couldn't breathe. Lori was on the loveseat. She would help me. I imagined being somewhere else, doing something else, anything else, but I was trapped. I kept hearing Lori breathing.

" 'I really like you,' Alfie whispered. Then he raped me.

"Why didn't I fight? Why am I just lying here wishing I were dead? When he was done, he got up and fumbled softly upstairs. Did his wife know? Would he hurt his new baby in the same way he hurt me? Tears thickened in the corners of my

eyes and dried there. Lori and I didn't talk. I heard her breathing and knew she was awake.

The next morning it was different between us, awkward; we couldn't laugh and play as we had yesterday. Alfie had ruined our friendship. A guilty flush reddened my face. *It was my fault. I must be to blame. Lori knows it. She knows I'm a tramp.*"

Donna moved from the easy chair to my sofa where I sat. She was silent, her eyes pained. "Yeah," I spat. "Alfie made me feel special, all right."

"What happened?"

"The weekend ended with everyone promising to get together soon, or write. Alfie and his wife invited me to come back and stay with them sometime. My grandparents thought the idea was great and gave them my Auntie Mae's phone number and address. 'Cheri will be staying here for a while, and I know she'd love to visit whenever you will have her.' *If only my grandma knew what 'have her' means to Alfie.* Staring at the ground, I forced a smile, quickly thanked them, and spun toward the car. As Alfie started toward the car, he stopped as I caught his eye, and we stared.

" 'She looks sad,' commented Grandma to Alfie and his wife. 'I don't think she wants to leave yet.' "

Donna winced. "Where did you go then?"

"We stayed at Lori's house, my Aunt Joyce's for two days. I would then go to Auntie Mae's house. My grandparents would leave for California. Now around Lori and her brother Craig, I felt I had to prove I was OK, so I entertained them. But even though I told jokes and goofed off, it wasn't fun. I felt uneasy, as if I was in a pressure cooker, sweating.

"Craig murmured to Lori, and she left the room. He eyed me like a cat and stalked intently around me, a bewildered mouse.

" 'Lori told me what you do and what happened at Alfie's house.' He pounced.

"The room swirled, mottling in ugly pasty colors. My head

burned, and I steadied myself with the wall, his voice zoning in and out. If I would perform oral sex on him, he would not tell anyone. I forced myself not to think. My mind blanked, and I did what I was told. My relationship with Craig was established that day. I did what he asked, never saying anything to anyone."

I looked deliberately at Donna. Her face was soft, uncondemning.

"A fog molded around me for the next couple days. Next thing I knew, I was at my Auntie Mae's house, and my grandparents were gone.

" 'We need to get that green off your teeth.' Auntie Mae shocked me into reality.

" 'No!' I had never noticed the greenish film that covered the tops of my teeth. 'Leave me alone,' I cried. No one had forced me to brush my teeth before. She used baking soda to scrub the green off. Yuck! It tasted terrible."

"Did you learn to like your new home?"

"My aunt was kind and tried to help me feel at home, but I hated being away from my family. "This is not my home! I want to go home!" I'd yell, my mind pounding with frustration. All I remember about my stay in Canada was I did everything possible to get home. At school, I refused to speak or do my work.

" 'She may be damaged emotionally by staying here,' the principal warned my aunt. 'Send her back to her parents if at all possible.'

"Auntie Mae agonized and prayed.

"During the time I was with her, almost a year, she took me to church every week, read to me, and took me on walks to the park. Her caring didn't matter. 'Please send me home,' I begged. Finally she agreed.

"*Yes! They'll miss me by now. Things will be normal. My mom and I will go out to breakfast sometimes. My sister will be near, and I'll have someone to share with.* Life took on a rosy-petaled glow, sweet with the thought of going home."

CHAPTER

10

You're not sharing my room,' my sister told me flatly when I arrived home. 'Don't you dare touch my stuff. If you even think about using my stereo, you're dead.' So much for a welcome. I was so thrilled to be back that I didn't care—much. I kept quiet because I didn't want to do anything to upset them so they'd send me back to Canada. A tight knot twisted in my stomach, but I was home. What was pain, anyway? I laughed, flippant.

"Weren't your parents at all glad to see you?" Donna spoke up again. She leaned forward in her chair, her chin resting on her knuckles. I scrunched my eyebrows and continued.

"One afternoon a week later, I was in the front yard playing with a friend when my sister's friend, Guy, came over. The three of us joked and laughed until Guy accidentally broke a piece of the fence bordering the driveway. He struggled to fix the fence, and I tried to help him. Just then my mom's boyfriend, Mac, pulled into the driveway. We froze.

"Mac looked at the fence and then at me, slamming the car door behind him. He curled his lip.

" 'The happiest days of our lives were when you were in Canada.' " He stormed inside. Everything inside me shriveled up and died. I knew that no matter what I did, I was bad, unlovable, and unwanted. Tears streamed down my face. I broke away from my friends and ran for my room.

" 'He didn't mean that . . . You know he doesn't mean that. He's just mad,' " I heard my friend calling after me. I wanted to believe her. But the truth was hard and cold and real. No one wanted me.

"I sat there in the deepening shadows in my tiny bedroom, the cold spreading numbness from my body to my heart."

Donna's face was bent in pain. I ground my fist in my hand. Donna straightened, her eyes dark pools.

"That was it. No more trying to get them to love me. I didn't need them or anyone. 'No one will ever be able to hurt me again,' I swore. No one would see my tears."

I walked to the window. " 'Can't you be more like your sister?' my family always asked. She was heavily into drugs, sexually active, and having a secret affair with a married man. If that's what they want, fine."

Donna shook her head. She looked down at her nails, struggling to say something. She didn't, and I kept on.

"Now in seventh grade, I befriended a group of kids who introduced me to drugs. At first the drugs made me euphoric. I felt no pain. I usually took too many and stumbled into walls and things. My favorite was a barbiturate, a sleeping pill, but I'd take anything, as long as it took the pain away. The side effects were confidence and well-being, a feeling I could do anything. The emotional pain I'd chalked up for years was gone when I was high."

"Did you get into trouble often at school?" Donna asked. She was with me, intent and encouraging.

"Not for being high. My skirts were too short, my makeup too heavy, or I just skipped school.

The Cheri Peters Story

" 'Why aren't you in school?' a man in his early thirties asked me on my way home one day.

" 'My skirt is only supposed to be three inches above my knee by our dress code. I was sent to the principal's office. He sent me home. I'm supposed to change into something more appropriate.'

" 'Your skirt is beautiful, and it looks great on you. Why don't you come in and have some soda. You don't have to go back to school. Forget about them.' He laughed.

" 'Yeah, forget about them.' My sarcasm felt good. I flounced across the street and into his house. I spent the afternoon watching movies, telling jokes, and wrestling on the floor."

Donna's eyes grew wide. A look of concern covered her face.

" 'My name's Dave, and I live here with my mother,' he said. 'My mean wife and I are getting a divorce.' He told me about his wife and their marriage. I felt sorry for him—and very grownup. He shared his feelings with me! Even things that made him sad. Wow! I had never felt special like that before.

"At the door, he kissed me. 'Thank you for listening to me. Will you come over again sometime?' I flushed, laughing, trying to sound grownup and failing miserably. He continued.

" 'I like you. I'd like to get to know you better.' Though I knew what 'I like you' could mean, I wasn't scared.

" 'I'll come over after school tomorrow,' I said, flattered.

" 'Great.'

"I thought about Dave all night. I wanted so desperately to be loved. Maybe he wouldn't love me, but he did like me, and we had fun. Dave warned me not to tell anyone, because if I did, we would get into trouble. 'They would not even let us see each other,' he mourned. I didn't say a word to my friends. When the school bell rang, I hurried toward Dave's house.

"Beep! Beep! I turned, and Dave's car pulled up next to me. We were off.

" 'I've got a surprise for you.'

" 'What? What is it?'

" 'You'll just have to wait,' he teased. On the other side of town, he pulled into an apartment complex.

" 'Close your eyes.' Dave opened my car door, picked me up, and carried me.

" 'This is our new apartment. Do you like it?'

" 'What do you mean 'our' new apartment. I don't understand. Did you rent this for us?'

" 'Yes. If we met at my mom's house, someone would find out. I couldn't bear not seeing you again. So I rented this place. Do you like it?'

" 'Yes, but it's just so weird.'

" 'Well, shut your eyes. I have another surprise for you.'

I shut my eyes, and Dave brought out champagne and flowers. That was the beginning of his seduction of me. For a long time he told me our relationship was special. That it didn't matter if we had sex or not, because he cared about me. I wanted to believe him. I was young, unloved, and incredibly damaged. I didn't understand how perpetrators, as they're called, can pick out a damaged child within minutes, use seduction so masterfully, how they create a dependency that is difficult to break or betray.'

Donna sighed. "Did you stay with him long?"

"Only until he had used me and got bored. I started taking more drugs on a regular basis. I hung out with kids who always partied and had a good time—or escaped a bad time. No matter how you look at it, it's ugly. The pattern repeats: Drugs, alcohol, party, sex. It was expected but now I was used to it. I'd remove myself totally from the situation by going someplace exciting in my mind. I usually blocked out a sexual encounter, unless it was overly abusive."

I looked at Donna. Was her love struggling, or was it getting weaker?

"I got pregnant. I had no idea whose baby it was. 'Don't worry.

The Cheri Peters Story

I'll marry you,' Wayne, one of my boyfriends, said. *Marry him? But I don't even love him.*

"When I tried to tell my mom, my tears erupted hot and violent.

" 'What's wrong?' Mom asked. Did she look concerned? 'Whatever it is, we can work it out.' I had never heard compassion from her before. I knew it wouldn't last.

" 'I'm pregnant.' I was twelve.

" 'Ha!" She hugged me. 'Is that all? I thought you had killed someone or something. It will all work out.'

Again I looked at Donna. Exhausted, I looked for the same disgust I felt toward myself in her eyes. She couldn't accept me, a tramp, not now. Her love couldn't reach where I'd fallen. Donna looked back, her face mirroring my pain, her warmth surrounded me. I turned to the window and started to cry. Her arms held me fast.

"I need a cigarette," I said.

"I need to go to the bathroom."

We both laughed.

CHAPTER 11

As I headed back to the family room, a tiny burst, like some dry crusty seed breaking open far below my surface, startled me. Was I beginning to trust her? She was being more real with me than she seemed to be with others. There was nothing phony in her love.

"Cheri," she said when she entered again. "I know I don't have the words to say. I'm afraid I'll say the wrong thing." Her eyes gazed far away. "But please believe me that Jesus won't. He understands, even when our minds struggle."

Her honesty filled me. "Thanks . . ." I broke off. *Did she want to hear more?*

"What happened with your pregnancy?"

"When the doctor came in long after my complicated delivery, I was smoking a cigarette. He glared at me, his voice cold. "You have all kinds of bad habits, don't you? Your twins are dead. The girl was stillborn and the boy just lived eight hours. A nurse will be in soon so you can fill the paperwork." He walked out. Although I was only thirteen, it devastated me.

The Cheri Peters Story

"Those babies were the only thing I had left. If no one else loved me, they would, us against the world. I laid there in the rumpled hospital bed and listened to the mother across the room feed her ten-pound newborn boy. She let me cradle him for a while. I stared at him, unbelievingly. Mine were dead.

"I wasn't asked if I was OK or how I felt. 'It's for the best,' I heard. 'You're so young.' 'It's God's will,' I heard another say. *God's will? Why would a God will something like this?* I tried not to let anyone see me cry or see my hurt.

" 'Now you won't marry me,' Wayne wailed. He stared at the empty crib in the hospital room, his face contorting in hysteria. 'Please, you'll still marry me, won't you?'

" 'It's OK. If you still want to get married, you'll have our support,' my mother said. Wayne's mother hedged. 'Sure.' I turned my head and stared blankly out the window facing a brick wall.

"Were you married?" Donna asked.

"Yes. I was thirteen. He was twenty-one. We were married in Mexico. I don't remember much about it. After the twins died, I just walked through life in a trance. I moved in with him and his mother. My family was happy. I had left home for good. Now that I was married, Wayne wouldn't leave me. Right? He joined the navy and moved overseas shortly after we married."

"He left that soon?" Donna's eyes widened.

" 'You ruined my son's life,' his mom told me. I endured two months living in yet another house that hated me. I had to get out. But where?

"I met a group of kids from Westlake Village, an affluent suburb. They had money, a car, and a cool yacht to live on. *This is the life*, I thought. Before long, their money was gone and they wanted to go home. I didn't have one, not where I belonged. Some of my friends let me move in with them and their parents, but I felt awkward. I knew I was not wanted there, but I stayed until I had the courage to leave. I had no idea where I was going to go from there. 'I want to go home,' I lied.

"They knew I didn't, but they dropped me off in Norwalk, close to my parents' house. Aimless, I started walking. I was truly on the streets now, nowhere to stay, nowhere to go. *Is this my future?* I was so afraid—afraid of being alone. I felt I was disappearing and no one seemed to notice. 'Hey, someone, anyone, can you still see me?' I wanted to scream. And no one would answer.

"A guy pulled over in a beat up yellow '62 T-bird. I smiled not at him but at the appearance of the car. Every part of the car seemed pieced together from another car. The doors were two different colors, one red, the other a golden yellow. One bumper was brown and the hood was tan. The guy leaned over the passenger seat and rolled down the window.

" 'Hey, where're you going?' "

" 'Don't know. Where are you going?' "

" 'To a party. There will be plenty of beer, pot, and fun. Want to come?' "

"I checked him out. He had long dark hair, straight nose, and a quick smile. He had a short goatee, and one ear was pierced. He seemed friendly enough. 'Sure!' What other options did I have?

" 'I'm Tommy,' he said as I hopped into his car.

"The party was nothing more than a number of addicts sitting around getting high. The people vegged on sagging sofas or sat cross-legged on the floor, getting high.

" 'You're so naive, little girl! You'll die on the street unless you're taught some things,' Tommy said when I told him my story. 'I'll educate you.' He took responsibility of my education, but in return, I had to take care of his sexual needs. This was never said out loud but understood, nevertheless. I told myself he loved me, but I never thought of how I felt for him. I never allowed myself to think—only react. It was easier that way. At twenty-eight, he was old for an addict. When younger, he'd con anyone out of or into anything, but his looks, health, and ability to con people were fading.

" 'You need to bring some money in,' Tommy said.

"My knuckles clenched white into fists. Getting a job for a girl on the street meant one thing. Prostitution. It would kill me.

" 'Please don't ask me to be a prostitute.'

"Tommy laughed. 'I'd never ask you to do that. I love you. What are you thinking? I know a man with a night club. You can work there as a waitress. We will get you an ID saying you are twenty-one.'

" 'Yeah, right. Who's going to believe I'm twenty-one?'

" 'Oh, they'll believe you. Leave everything to me. I know these guys. They like young girls.' I bit my lip and tried to relax.

"Within a week I scheduled an interview at the club and had the proper ID. As I got dressed for the interview, no matter how I tried, I looked thirteen. I caked on heavy makeup, curled my long blond hair, and wore a low-cut black dress. My hands sweated, and my knees shook.

" 'Relax!' Tommy said. 'You already have the job. They just want to meet you.'

" 'Little Abners. Nude Dancers,' a painted sign hung in front of the small, dirty bar.

" 'I will not dance nude!' I shrieked.

" 'You will.' Tommy exploded, grabbing my arm in a tight squeeze. His voice slammed into me. 'You have to do something, and this is no big deal once you get used to it. You don't have to have sex with anyone, just walk around a stage with your clothes off. You don't even need to know how to dance.'

"I had never seen him so mad. Fear, not that he would hit me—that was no big deal, but that he'd leave me, stifled me. Tommy meant security, a place to stay even if it was sleeping in the car. *Please don't leave me!*

" 'OK,' I whispered.

"Inside, my eyes strained to adjust to the dimly lighted room. A few scruffy men lounged around a small stage area with mirrored walls. A young girl, maybe sixteen, was dancing for an old man holding up some money. One guy turned and stared at me, his eyes leering and curious. Like in a bad dream, my legs itched to run, but I couldn't.

" 'Don't worry. You'll be nervous for a while, but that will pass,' the owner said. 'You're very pretty. You should make a lot of money.' Tommy brightened up. He gave me some uppers, we both downed tequila, and the owner handed me a skimpy girl scout costume to wear on stage.

" 'You can start now.'

"I changed into the tiny costume in the drab changing room. *Now?* My heart did backflips, breathing hurt, and my palms were sweating. *I'm a famous dancer auditioning for the star role*, I imagined. *I am confident, talented, successful. Now move.* My feet thumped slowly onto the wooden stage. I froze.

" 'Just walk around!' I heard Tommy say, his voice hung suspended, distant. I tried to smile and walked back-and-forth across the stage, but my tears smarted and blurred my eyes. My stomach felt like batter, beat by the stench of cigarettes, alcohol, and a damp, moldy smell. I looked for Tommy, but the lights glared onto the stage, blinding me. *Get me out of here.* The old man seen earlier waved something green in the air trying to get me closer. I walked over, and he dropped the money on the floor in front of me. He didn't see my tears. No one seemed to notice. Shutting my eyes, I lifted my hands and slowly moved to the music. I was a beautiful ballet dancer.

"The music stopped, jarring me to the cold present. I kept my eyes shut.

" 'Hey, go get that money all over the floor,' the owner called. I picked up the money, ignoring the old man making disgusting gestures with his tongue. Seventy-three dollars. Tommy grinned."

The Cheri Peters Story

Donna shifted in her chair. She looked sad. "Did you get used to the job like they said?"

"It took a long time and a lot of drugs. The club hired me full time. I never looked into their faces, which helped. I gave the money I made to Tommy. When he was happy, I felt safe."

"What did he do with the money? Drugs?"

"Yeah, mostly. A group of us hung out, staying sometimes in funny places, sometimes on the street, in cheap motels, a drug house, or a crash pad. Everyone pitched in what money they earned to help."

I glanced at Donna. She led a sheltered, clean, and innocent life. How could she stand to listen to this? Shame filled me, and I closed my eyes.

"Please go on," Donna said.

"One place we shacked out in was The California Hotel. It was just four dollars a night, but after buying drugs for ten to fifteen people, we could barely manage that. A small bed filled most of the dirty room, dark curtains covered a tiny cobwebbed window. Drug paraphernalia lay scattered around. If you were lucky, there'd even be some useable syringes with maybe just a slight burr on the needletip that could be filed down and reused.

"I watched as the group prepared the drug. Everyone hunched over the nightstand, mesmerized, as Tommy heated the heroin in a spoon by placing a match flame beneath it. The drug, a subtle charmer, hypnotized them, leaving them eager and mindless. *It must really work.* Once the drug was strained through some cotton or whatever could be found, it was drawn up into a syringe and injected.

" 'Can I try it too?' I asked Tommy.

" 'Forget it. Heroin will place a monkey on your back that you'd never be able to get off.'

" 'Come on. Everyone else is doing it. I feel left out.'

" 'No!' His hand sent me reeling. This was the only thing that he'd hit me for.

"To escape these exhibitions, I often groped down the dark hall to the dilapidated bathroom, my heart hammering. This hotel didn't draw the best clientele, and I felt vulnerable. People I met in the broken hallway looked evil. 'Walk tall and no eye contact,' Tommy had coached me on survival. Once locked inside, I sometimes wanted to sleep in there, but the smell soon sent me gagging to the room."

"Did you ever sleep outside?" Donna asked. Her face looked slightly green.

"I slept in a park once. The stars overhead, the clean smell of flowers, bushes, and trees. It was incredible . . . until the darkness of early morning when the sprinklers came on. I jumped up, but by the time I escaped, I was wet and cold."

"Since you spent so much time with your group, did you ever get close to them?" Donna asked.

"No. While I got to know everyone, no one could ever get close. If you were there and needed something, they'd help, but if you were gone, forget it. People come and go. Some would move on to something else, some would try to clean up, some would get busted and go to jail.

"In this environment, I was ultra-aware of everything. I had to be. If a fight broke out, people would literally yank out pipes from under the sink, break off table legs, or use whatever else was in reach as a weapon. I can't count the times I frantically blotted a gaping wound to stop the bleeding on some guy just stabbed or beaten."

Donna winced. "That must have been scary."

"Nah, what scared me was being left alone. The police broke in during one of these fights. They handcuffed Tommy. *Why?* I wondered. I couldn't go outside to ask any questions for fear they'd pick me up as a runaway. No one was looking for me, but I was too young.

" 'Don't go. Don't take him,' I cried as he was shoved into the back seat of the police car.

" 'Tommy was arrested for outstanding warrants,' a guy named Billy came in to tell me. 'He said that you're to stay with me 'til he gets out of jail.'

" 'You? How long is he in jail for?'

" 'Could be six months. They found a lot of warrants.' He smiled.

"Where did you come from? Why are you smiling like that? But I just said, 'Where are you staying?' I wished Tommy was here to tell me it was OK.

" 'With a friend. You're now with me.' Billy grabbed my arm. 'Get your things and let's go before the police come back.'

"Are you two ever going to stop talking?" Jake asked, coming into the room. Donna and I laughed. Jake had left us to talk all this while, and I appreciated it.

"Hey, do you want to take a walk with me? I'd like to move around," I said.

"Not now. I'm in the middle of a game. Just wanted to check on you. How 'bout later?" He headed back for the kitchen.

"Yeah," I said, disheartened. I got up to stretch my legs.

"I would love to go with you," Donna said. "The fresh air would feel good. I just need to put on my hiking shoes. I'll be right out."

I went outside to wait for her. I lighted a cigarette, inhaling the herbs deeply. Ugly pictures stormed my head. These memories bombarded me, clear and blasting memories I'd been able to stuff away for years. Even though these stories repulsed Donna, they couldn't compare to the real thing or even to vivid pictures now filling my mind, like gray, falling ash. I looked up at the blue horsetail cloud sky. Would He hear me? Who was He anyway?

"Lord, you gotta help me through this."

CHAPTER

12

Donna's house was perched on a pine-wooded hill at the base of the Sierras. The ragged rock peaks zigzagged up to regal glaciers, distant and gleaming. Dark green strokes of trees brushed upward on brown, finally meeting a white-sponged sky. The beauty took my breath away . . . or was it my cigarette. I couldn't tell which. Donna and I hiked along a pebbled path meandering into the forest. The warm breeze was tangy with needles. A steller's jay flapped to a higher branch, quivering it. A fly buzzed by, and a chipmunk trilled from a decaying stump ahead. We walked, breathing pungent sap and crunching pine cones. I soon gasped for breath. Donna, active, vegetarian—in her early fifties, often had to wait up for me—young twenty-three. The drugs and cigarettes wreaked havoc on my body. She could hike circles around me, but she was patient.

"So what was this guy like that dragged you off? What happened next?" Donna asked.

"Billy and his friends weren't much different from Tommy's gang, except for one thing. Billy forbade me to go outside during daylight. None of his reasons made sense.

Billy consumed an astonishing amount of drugs and alcohol, and I amazed him because I could keep up. We were drugged out all the time. I fell in love with LSD, acid, Billy's favorite drug because this hallucinogenic kept me high longer. One tab of acid could keep me tripping for twelve hours. I took thirty-five tabs in a week. I'd pass out once in awhile and call that sleep.

Billy disgusted me. Under his scowling, leathered face, he wasn't bad looking, but he dressed sleazy, and his face was always tense. If he'd relax, smile once in awhile, trash some of his anger, he'd be kind of cute. Sometimes I felt sorry for him. He seemed so lost, so unconnected to anyone or anything. I, at some level, understood him. It didn't matter if he spooked me. He liked me, and we had a place to stay. The drugs calmed my uneasiness.

One night Billy's friend asked us to watch his studio apartment while he was gone. We needed a place to crash, so it worked great. The door of the tiny apartment opened into a dark, filthy living area with a bed, a TV sitting on a cardboard box, and a small refrigerator with a hot plate on top. When my shoes stuck to the bathroom floor, I almost threw up. The place gave me the creeps. So did Billy, when I wasn't high.

"Billy flopped on the bed and ranted for hours about the police, his family, and how bad women were. *Please just shut up and go to sleep.* Billy raged on, finally passing out around three. Physically and mentally exhausted, in the relieving silence I drifted off to sleep.

"*KABOOM!* Like a bomb, the studio door exploded, splinters flying. The room burst with police, riot guns pointed at us. There were at least 12 officers, some in uniforms, some dressed in plain clothes.

" 'On the floor, NOW. I said NOW. On the floor and put your hands behind your back. NOW.'

"Shock paralyzed me. What in the world?

"I was slammed to the floor.

" 'So, Billy, did you think we wouldn't find you?' Obscenities flew thick.

"A plainclothes officer yanked my face up so he could see me. 'How old are you? How old is she, Billy? thirteen, fourteen?'

"Billy lay there, not saying a word.

" 'Let's see, murder, escape, what should we charge here? Molestation, statutory rape on a minor? You have just bought yourself some more trouble.' He turned to the other officers and laughed. They joined him.

" 'And you,' he squatted down in front of me. 'You . . . Do you know who you're with? This guy is wanted. He has recently escaped from prison. Do you know what he was in prison for?' He grabbed my face and peered into my eyes. 'For murdering his wife.' His voice got louder, 'For thirteen, you keep great company. Look at yourself lying on the floor naked with a murderer, surrounded by the police. Your parents would be so proud,' he spat.

"My parents couldn't care less. Murder? Escaped from prison? I knew something was weird, but I never thought I could be killed.

"While the police ransacked the studio, searching, I lay cold and naked on the floor. When they found a few hits of acid and alcohol, we were arrested.

" 'You have the right to remain silent. If you give up the right to remain silent, anything you say can be used against you in a court of law . . . Do you understand? I asked you a question. Do you understand?'

" 'Yes,' we said together.

" 'Get some clothes on. It is disgusting to see such a young girl prostituting herself out. How does it feel to be a prostitute at thirteen? How does it feel to be used up at thirteen? Get dressed.'

The Cheri Peters Story

"I seethed. *I am fourteen and not a prostitute. I am not used up. I hate you for being so mean.* I grabbed my clothes and stalked to the bathroom to get dressed.

" 'No—get dressed here. Are you suddenly shy? How sweet. You can have sex with a convict who you barely know, and you want me to believe you somehow have morals? Just get dressed. You disgust me.' "

" 'I hate you.' I said under my breath. I was livid. How dare he talk to me like this. He doesn't even know me. He knows nothing about my life or where I've come from or what choices I have . . . or don't have.

" 'What did you say?' He stepped closer to me.

"I couldn't look at him. My heart heaved to my throat. *You can't scare me. You can't scare me. You can't* . . . I shivered in a cold sweat.

" 'Do you realize I probably saved your life? Or are you too stupid to even understand that? You should be thanking me, but instead you say you hate me. I'm hurt.' Laughter.

"I stared at Billy, his hands cuffed to a belt secured around his waist, his ankles cuffed too. Would he have killed me too?

"His angry look was foul and answered my question.

" 'Get him out of here.' The plainclothes officer said to the others, 'I'll bring her down.'

" 'No! Don't leave me with this ——.' It was useless to say.

" 'It's Officer McMillan. You don't want to go with me, but you'd go with him?' he said, pointing to Billy. 'You are really something. I am awed by your judgment.'

" 'Let's go.' He handcuffed me.

"Outside, police cars swarmed the parking lot, the street, and even the sidewalk, parked at various angles. Never had I seen so many in one place. *Uh-oh. I'm really in trouble.*

"Officer McMillan led me to an unmarked car, opened the door, and pushed the top of my head down as I was shoved in the front seat. He walked to his side and climbed in.

"I thought of many names I'd like to call Officer McMillan, but none of them were his.

"We rode in silence for a few miles.

" 'What were you doing with him?' he blew up.

"I stared straight ahead.

" 'Is this the way you're going to start your life? Are you going to run around with—no, sleep around with—murderers and drug addicts? Do you realize that you will either end up dead or a worn-out prostitute by the time you're sixteen?' He didn't wait for me to reply. 'I could tell you stories about girls a lot smarter than you that ended up dead, dead at sixteen. Is that what you want?' he shouted.

"I glared at him, anger flaring inside. I opened my mouth, but before I said anything, I saw a tear slide down his cheek. I couldn't speak. What? Did he care about me? About the people he busted? Why? I wanted to say something, but I just sat there.

"Arriving at the station, I was fingerprinted, photographed, and placed in a small holding cell. Not so bad, I thought. Tommy's been through this a hundred times. I had not.

"The door opened, and a female officer came in. 'I'm going to check you for paraphernalia. Take your clothes off.'

" 'Why do I have to take my clothes off?' sarcasm peaked in my voice.

" 'It is our policy to check all orifices for paraphernalia,' she said professionally. I was humiliated.

" 'Where do you live?'

" 'With my dad in Long Beach,' I lied.

" 'Does he know where you were last night?'

" 'No. I ran away. He has no idea where I am,' I said, hoping they would call him to come get me. I wasn't sure whether he would or not, or if he'd go along with my lie. I took my chances. I couldn't be in any more trouble.

" 'What is your dad's phone number?' she asked.

" 'I forgot.' She raised her eyebrows.

The Cheri Peters Story

"It seemed like forever before I heard footsteps approaching my cell again. I sat up. 'We've found your father, and he's on the way to the station to pick you up,' the female officer said in a monotone voice. *Does she want to reassure me?*

"My dad played his role, the concerned parent, perfectly. However, when they pressured him to press statutory rape charges against Billy, he refused.

" 'She went with him willingly, and she's in trouble all the time. I'd rather focus on getting her help than pursue charges against this guy.' The officers looked angry.

"We left the station. I couldn't believe they'd just released me to my dad. Our conversation was shallow but pleasant, and he dropped me at a friend's place.

" 'Thanks for getting me out of jail.' He tried to kiss me, but I jumped out of the car."

I looked at Donna. We had stopped to rest as I was telling my story. She was sitting on a rock, her knees drawn up and her hands clasped around them. The sun was shining on her silvered hair, and the breeze played with flyaway strands. She had listened a long time, without interruption. Her eyes were wide.

"I can't believe what a mess I was . . ." I looked down at my feet. ". . . I am."

"How could you be anything other than that with the history you've had?" Her eyes were soft. "The more I listen, the more I'm amazed you look as good as you do. It's amazing you are still alive."

My throat caught. *No, what's amazing is that you are here, Donna, helping me to heal.* A strange warmth seeped inside. *Who is this woman? Who is this God that she believes in?*

73

CHAPTER 13

"Did Tommy ever get out of jail?" We were walking back from our hike.

"Yes, but he was arrested again on drug charges and transferred to a minimum security "ranch" for a year. I was on the streets alone again, no place to stay."

"How did you survive?" Donna asked.

"I lived on a kind of automatic pilot. I trained myself to not think or ask questions at all. Usually that helped. After all, who wants to understand why you're being raped . . . again or why someone died or always wonder if you're going to have a place to stay or food tomorrow, even today? I taught myself to respond to *now*."

"That makes sense," Donna nodded understandingly.

"Taking care of myself terrified me, but I always hid how I felt and looked in control. *How do I find a place to stay, get enough food, enough drugs?* I didn't know how safe Tommy kept us or what common sense he had, but I felt safe near him. Now he was in jail again."

"Did you go back to Tommy's friends?"

"For awhile I hung out with them, but I had to move on."

"Why?"

"The biggest reason was I was an attractive young female and the other girls, the oldest around sixteen, felt threatened with me around. Jealousies and arguments grew more and more intense. For one, Tommy always sheltered me while the other girls prostituted themselves and robbed stores and houses. I was being taken care of."

"Taken care of?" Donna asked, stopping on the trail. I looked at Donna and laughed. She chuckled.

"I would not wish that kind of care. . . ."

With no warning, black sobs burst through my body, a flashflood with no control. I had seen such ugly stuff at only fourteen. Couldn't I flush these memories down the toilet? My education on the streets was so thorough. I was so dirty, such trash. *Don't waste your effort on me, Donna.*

I quieted. "Do you think God still loves me?"

"Yes." She held me for the longest time.

We walked back to the house.

"I need a cigarette."

"I need to use the bathroom."

After I finished my cigarette, I joined Donna in the family room. She put on soft piano music on the stereo. What was this strange warmth I felt? Was it trust? *No! Yuck!* My thoughts recoiled. *Never! I will never trust you. Never. So you're nice, so you've listened, but you're not for real. You, too, will prove a fake. There is no one I can trust.* Some crazy love was peeking, throwing its seeds in through a crack in my thick emotional walls. *Quit it. I'll only add more bricks if you try to get inside. I will never let you in. As soon as I believe you, you will disappear. All that has ever seemed good was not. The love will not really be love and the concern not really true. Why can't you be real? Oh, I need you to be real.*

Donna's voice, gentle and far away, pulled me back from my thoughts. *Huh, what?* Something of her own inconsistencies. I refocused slowly. *What was she thinking?*

"... Oh, I know the love and forgiveness of Jesus Christ, but often I find myself acting the exact opposite of what I know and have experienced from God. It's so shaming. Paul, one of my favorite writers from the Bible, agonized about this very thing. He cried out, "Wretched man that I am! Who will deliver me from this body of death? Thanks be to God through Jesus Christ our Lord" (Romans 7:24, 25, RSV). It seemed Donna could read my mind and see my fears.

"People may not always be able to do or say the right thing, because of their own struggles with sin or with past damage, and I know that I'm not worthy of anyone's trust. But Jesus is, and He will always love us, and He will always say the right thing. The Bible warns us to not look at each other for salvation but to look only at Jesus. He will never let us down, and even though we must struggle and wade through ugly messes in this life, He will always be with us. He will show us the way to get through all this darkness."

My jaw quivered. "How do you know? You seem so perfect. And I don't see how you can accept me."

"Cheri, listen. You must look only to Jesus, not to me for acceptance. I'm human and can make mistakes." She shared her own weaknesses. "My mother was very judgmental, making it difficult for me to accept others, especially men." *You? Unaccepting? Spare me.* Her sharing surprised me. "Cheri, I'm just like you, a sinner saved by grace."

"Ha. Come on. Do you expect me to believe that your sins are as bad as mine?" I bit my tongue. "How can Jesus love someone like me? It doesn't make sense."

Donna's eyes glowed with a truth so alluring; her smile was gentle, real, and just for me. "The Bible clearly states that we all are sinners in desperate need of a Saviour. The good news is that Jesus died for our sins, all of our sins. No one is excluded."

"I wish I could believe that," I whispered more to myself than Donna.

"It's true." We both sat listening to the quiet music. I closed my eyes, her words echoing in my head. Then she laughed out loud.

"What's so funny?"

"I have to tell you something. I hope I can explain it right. I really want to show you God's love. But it's not easy for me. I really want to help you see how much Jesus loves and accepts you. How he searched for you like a lost sheep until He found you, never giving up. How all of heaven waits breathlessly for you to see how much the Lord loves you. How they will all celebrate when you accept His love."

My tears welled.

"But it's not easy for me . . . so I keep going into the bathroom to pray and ask God to help me. To help me to not say the wrong thing, to accept and love you unconditionally because that is the way God loves us. I walk in there and fall on my knees. I do not want to show you me but to show you only Jesus."

"I thought you had a kidney problem. I have never met anyone that had to go to the bathroom as much as you," I sniffed. We both laughed.

She prayed for me? Wow! My amazement knotted into fear. This crazy love had not just thrown seeds inside my walls, one had sprouted. *Was the enemy inside? Was it now me? Could I not trust myself?* An awkward silence grew.

"Are you thirsty?"

"Yes, do you have anything caffeinated?" I smiled, knowing she did not and that she knew I knew. As we walked into the kitchen, my stomach growled.

Jake, with his nephew and neice, were still in the dining room playing Uno. *That must be a really wild game,* I thought. Sitting with them while we ate, it was fun to listen to them tease and razz each other.

"Do you and Cheri want to join us?"

"No. Card games aren't for me," Donna said.

"No, thanks." I still felt too stupid to play a game, especially without being high.

"I'll clean up," I offered. Donna joined me in the kitchen. *This is normal stuff.* A family playing games, eating together, and cleaning up. In my childhood, my parents ate in the living room and we kids always in the kitchen.

I finished the dishes in silence, unaware of what Donna was doing, lost in my own thoughts. When I walked back to the family room, Donna had put new music in.

"The singers are twins," she said, handing me the tape cover. I looked at a picture of two smiling sisters. Sadness swept over me. *I will never have that kind of closeness with my sisters. The damage in our family encouraged us to compete, never love each other. I don't know how to change. I don't know if I can handle this change, this recovery. Man, I want some drugs!* The physical pains of the withdrawal were becoming manageable, but a deeper, emotional pain was awakening. Like after an accident, the shock was wearing away, the throbbing ache beginning.

"Lord, help me."

"What did you say?" Donna asked.

"Oh, I'm sorry. I was just thinking out loud. This is going to be harder than I thought." I smiled. I don't know why. It was all I could do to keep from screaming, running desperately away. But to what? *How am I going to come out of this? Will I be able to do a simple task without feeling so much sadness, regret, and pain? Will I ever feel normal? Be normal? Whatever that is?*

"Whatever happened to you after you left Tommy's friends?" Donna asked. She sensed I needed a break from my pounding thoughts.

CHAPTER 14

Luck was on my side because a local drug dealer took an interest in me. His name was Jimmy Speed. He was a short, wiry guy with dark, oily hair. He may have been a nice-looking boy, but the drugs had taken their toll on him. While he gave me a place to stay, Jimmy Speed was scary. Sometimes he'd be high on speed for days on end without sleep, food, or water. He'd do nothing but pop pills. His eyes got glassy, he'd get incredible facial ticks and distortions, and his body would jerk, like a seizure but smoother, more snakelike. In paranoia, he thought people were out to kill him. Man, he could be danger-ous. It was hard for me to bring him down, to convince him he was safe.

"One night Jimmy and a friend sat laughing in the kitchen, carving Xs on the top of saccharine tablets.

" 'We just found out that the guy who asked to buy a couple of jars of whites is an undercover narcotics officer. We're going to sell him these sugar tablets instead of the drugs. They won't be able to do nothing to us,' they guffawed.

"*I wish Tommy was out of jail*. Life was like walking on shattered glass. Jimmy and his friend carved pills all night, and in the early afternoon, they left to sell their bogus drugs to the police. I went to work at the bar and came back around 3:00 a.m. The house was still. To my delight, no one was home. Wow! I hadn't had time to myself in a long time. I took a hot bath and went to bed.

"I woke to excruciating pain. Something smashed my face, but my eyes stuck shut. Slam! I tasted blood on my lip. I brought my hands up to cover my face, but too slow. Another blow. I tried to twist over onto my stomach, but a heavy weight trapped my legs. I heard yelling, but couldn't make anything out. Then I was wrenched out of bed. Who were these guys?

" 'Where is he? Where is Jimmy?' a man in a black leather jacket yelled. His face mottled with rage, and he shook. He mashed me onto the ground and kicked me in the chest.

" 'I don't know where Jimmy is,' I cried, dragging myself into a corner. I squinted through a puffy eye. Two men. One was blond, muscled, and furious. The other was taller, dark-haired, and calmer. He seemed uneasy with the other's rage. *Who are these guys?*

" 'I have no idea. I don't mess in Jimmy's stuff,' " I said to the dark-haired man.

" 'Shut up.' The blond kicked me again two or three times.

"I tried to catch my breath. He grabbed me by the hair and threw me into the closet doors. He turned around and began hurling dresser drawers on the floor.

" 'Search everything,' he yelled. He glared at me. 'You either tell me where he is or you are going to jail.'

"*Jail?* Then it all made sense. These were the undercover narcotics officers that Jimmy sold the bogus drugs to. Icy fear cut me, nearly slicing me in two. I couldn't call the police. They were the police. And they were out of control.

"The two guys tore the apartment apart, yelling constantly,

threatening jail. They dumped everything onto the floor and pawed through all the drawers, cupboards, and closets. Whether Jimmy had any drugs in the apartment or not, I didn't know. But these men might plant some if they didn't find any.

" 'OK. We've found paraphernalia, a waterpipe,' the blond said. The waterpipe was a wine bottle made into a pipe for smoking marijuana.

" 'Hey, that was bought only for display and never used for smoking anything,' I protested. The blond officer threw me into the bedroom.

" 'Get dressed. You're under arrest.'

"Dressing, I gasped at my reflection in the mirror. A huge reddened area swelled the right side of my face, one eye was swollen shut, and my lip was split open. My body felt as bad as my face looked. The blond jerked me from my stare and handcuffed me.

"They booked me into the Orange County Jail, a process taking several hours. The shock worn off, pain plastered me, and my entire body screamed at the wrongful beating. I knew better than to tell the truth about what had happened, so I kept silent.

" 'The waterpipe was a decoration bought at a head shop. It's never been used for drugs,' I only repeated. After a complete body search, they threw me in a cell with a few older women. *How in world will I get out of this one?*

" 'Come on. You're being bailed out,' the jailer said, motioning me up the next morning." 'What? Who would bail me out?' On the street, people don't take care of each other like that. If you're gone one day, people might talk about you for a while, but nothing more. *This is weird*, I puzzled. I quietly followed the officer down the corridor and into the office."

CHAPTER

15

A distinguished-looking older man with a gray suit and floral tie rose to meet me as I stumbled in, his hand extended. He reminded me of my grandfather from Oklahoma, silver hair and soft voice.

" 'Hello. I'm an attorney from Newport Beach.' He shook my hand. *An attorney? For me?* 'I heard about your case, and I'm outraged by what has happened.'

" 'Uh, oh?' I waited for the catch. *What does this man want from me?*

" 'Let's go to my office and discuss what we can work out for you.' He led me, dazed, from the police station. As I was passing through the huge lobby of his office, the secretary smiled. I stared at the plants, the vaulted ceilings, the engraved polished door. Inside his office, books from floor to ceiling were packed in a beautiful built-in oak bookcase. The light brown carpet was so plush that my feet sank into it. I sank into a white leather armchair and savored the rich comfort.

" 'We're going to need evidence of your attack,' the lawyer

said, drawing out a camera. 'May I take pictures of the bruises on your face and body? This is evidence of the violence.'

" 'Go ahead.' I glanced over at a gold-gilded mirror. I shrank from the skinny, freckled girl staring back. The reddened areas I'd seen yesterday swelled with more colors today, dark purple, black, and yellow. My lip was fat, with dried blood on it, and my eye was crusty and puffed. I looked as if I'd been dragged from a war.

" 'Why do we need evidence?'

" 'To sue the county, the owners of the building for letting the police in with their pass key, and the police department.'

" 'Sue the police?' The idea shocked me. Yeah. So what do you want from me? I waited in silence. He explained the steps we needed to take.

" 'Please explain in detail what took place the night you were arrested,' he said, pulling out an elegant fountain pen from his front pocket. As I talked, he wrote, then gave me forms to sign.

" 'Do you need any money?'

" 'What?' That got my attention.

" 'You have a sure thing with this lawsuit. When this whole thing is over, you'll have plenty of money.'

" 'But that's when it's over.'

" 'Yes. But if you need any now, I would gladly give you a loan, an advance.' He smiled.

" 'I do need some money to help out with the rent. How much could you loan me?' *This is too good to be true.*

" 'How would one hundred dollars be?' I gulped as he reached into his pocket and pulled out a crisp one-hundred-dollar bill.

" 'That's fine.' I eyed him suspiciously. Who is this guy? I thought, as I signed for the money. He must want something. He drove me back to my apartment. He didn't try to do anything to me.

" 'If you think of anything new, please call me, immediately,' he said.

"I heard from my attorney often within the next few months. He talked about the lawsuit as if we'd already won. 'This is too easy,' he'd say. He stopped asking me if I needed any money and just gave it. He sometimes gave fifty, one hundred, and once even three-hundred dollars. *Wow! This is great.* I basked in the ease. One thing made me squirm. Was I becoming dependent on him?

" 'Don't worry. It's really your own money, and when the lawsuit is won, you will pay me back,' he'd assure me. I believed him.

"Jimmy, never caught, started selling drugs for a major player in the area.

" 'Why can't I go with you?' I asked once, when Jimmy headed for the dealer's house.

" 'Because the guy's paranoid about newcomers. He'd freak out if you tagged along.'

When, after a long time, Jimmy let me come, I understood the need for careful screening. A large amount of drugs and money went through that house, and the dealer also dealt with a huge volume of stolen goods—from cars to cameras. In amazement, I once watched the dealer and his crew bury a stolen car.

"One day while I was alone at Jimmy's place, someone knocked on the door. Opening the door, I faced the dealer, his face impassive. *What now?*

" 'What do you want?' I asked. He pushed his way past me, grim and silent. Turning, he pulled a gun from his coat and shoved it an inch from my face. My knees buckled, and my head fogged.

" 'I just got out of jail. Someone snitched on me, and my house was raided by the police. Do you know anything about that?' He didn't pause. 'If it was you that turned me in, I'll kill you, and not only you, but your family.'

" 'But I . . .' He pulled out a small notebook and began to read addresses of family members. I gasped. 'Why me?'

The Cheri Peters Story

"He shut the notebook and glared at me intently. 'You were the latest person allowed to come over. You were just arrested, so you probably gave me up to save yourself. The raid on my house was thorough, and the police knew everything, including the buried stuff.'

" 'I didn't say anything to anyone. I swear! I don't know who turned you in, but it wasn't me. Please don't hurt my family. Please find out for sure who did it. It wasn't me.' I was rambling, and my mind blurred.

" 'When I find out who's to blame, they'll be killed.' He left. I sank to the floor and stared at the wood paneling. What do I do? Wait? Impossible. What if he couldn't get to the bottom of things. What if he just went on his hunches?

" 'This dealer has people that'll find out for him who the police informant was, and then he'll be taken care of,' Jimmy assured me that night. I felt like a player in a low-grade gangster movie. My mind ticked a hundred tocks per second."

I'm sick of being scared all the time. It's dumb to sue the police. I've seen movies where the police just killed a drug addict for no reason. That blond officer would have. Now I have a drug dealer who thinks I snitched on him to the police. If he only knew, I'd never trust the police after what happened to me. And if this isn't bad enough, I'm living with a paranoid speed freak who thinks everyone's out to get him.

" 'Phone call.' Jimmy interrupted my mad thoughts. 'It's your attorney.'

"I took the phone. 'Yes?'

" 'Cheri, we really have to talk. The lawsuit may have to be dropped. I am not sure we can win after all.'

" 'What? Why?' My world screeched to a stop. Would this nightmare never end?

" 'It looks like your history of drug abuse, and definitely Jimmy's, complicates things. We also have to deal with the "statute of limitations," which means we can't even file after a certain date passes. I'm getting a lot of heat from some pretty high places too. It looks like we're going to have to figure something out fast.'

"Dependent on his money, I cringed. Most of the time, he paid my share of the rent and gave me spending money.

" 'Your loans will have to stop until we decide for sure which way this lawsuit is going to go. Can I come over to talk?

" 'Sure.' My mind was freaking. What am I going to do?

" 'We'll go out to lunch,' he said, and hung up.

"The restaurant on the beach overlooked foaming crests and a curling cove. Seagulls swooped over blue-green waves ribboned with white sand, but I couldn't enjoy the view. My attorney talked about the lawsuit, the year in general, and how much he had grown fond of me. I picked at my food. What would I do now without this money? What did he want?

" 'I can't just leave you without any means of support,' he said, real concern in his voice. 'I have a friend who can help you for a while. Until you can get on your feet. Do you want to meet her?'

" 'Yes, sure.' I said simply. *But why does he care?* I didn't have any real job skills, but maybe she would train me.

"We arrived at an expensive, beautiful condominium in Newport Beach. 'This is Sandy,' my attorney introduced me at the door, then quickly left. Sandy, an older woman in a professional suit, bright lipstick and heavy earrings, smiled at me and welcomed me in. What would I be doing? A receptionist? A maid for this ritzy place? I couldn't imagine.

" 'This is an incredible job opportunity for you,' " she said. 'You will make a lot of money, because you're so pretty and young.' I froze inside. 'Let me explain the business.'

"*Oh, God, get me out of here!* I'd been set up by my attorney. Sandy and a group of attorneys ran a child prostitution ring. *I can't do this!*

" 'The split will be 60/40 at first,' she was saying. 'If you work hard, you could eventually earn 75 percent.' She stopped, a big smile of reassurance. 'You'll do really well!' Stunned, nausea left me speechless. 'Your first trick, your customer, is on the way. I have to leave because the tricks don't like to be seen by many people. I'll be back later.' She left, a cloud of perfume, firmness, and finality.

"I gagged at the job description. How am I going to get out of here? I ran to the window, not knowing what to do. The door was locked. Where was I? Did I have time to escape? I looked frantically for a phone, with no success. Where's a knife? I grew desperate.

"Ding-dong. My heart jammed, then tried to break right out of my chest."

CHAPTER

16

I won't answer the door. I held my breath in case he could hear me breathing from outside. *Please go away!*

" 'Is anyone there? Please open the door.'

"A key jiggled in the lock, the doorknob turned slowly. There was no place to run.

" 'I'm sorry. I didn't think anyone one was here. Didn't you hear me ring the bell?' said a tall man in his late fifties.

" 'No, I didn't hear you.' My mouth was so dry I could barely speak.

" 'It's all right. I am in now. What is your name?'

"I bit my lip. I wouldn't tell him my name. I would never tell him anything. He walked over to me and sat down beside me. He looked like a doctor or something, not like someone who would ask the services of a prostitute, especially a child. I felt sick.

" 'Are you afraid? Nervous?' He sounded professional.

" 'Yes. I don't want to do this,' I whispered.

" 'It's too late. I have already paid for you.' His voice was soft, trying to sound understanding. He slowly undressed himself and then me, my mind still frozen.

"Suddenly, with more strength than I thought I had, I screamed. He stopped.

" 'I am not going to do this. Please leave. Please leave now!' The man obeyed, angry and silent. I was amazed.

"I gathered my clothes and got dressed. I left a note for Sandy and my attorney: 'Sorry, I cannot do this.' I felt stupid and sick. Why am I so easy to take advantage of? I will never trust anyone or be so stupid again. I walked out to the main street. Which way to go now? I stuck out my thumb. So much for not trusting or being stupid.

Donna listened, her shoulders tense and her knuckles white in her folded hands.

"Whew," she sighed. "Where did you end up next?"

"Back with Tommy, who was finally released from jail."

"You really must have felt safe with him."

"Well, safer than on my own. He bought a car for fifty dollars, so we had a place to sleep for a while."

"Did you ever find an apartment?"

"Yes. With Tommy in the works again, our old gang was back: Big Bob, Angie, DeeDee, Johnny, Rick. Together, we rented a cheap apartment, because Big Bob, though on probation at work, still had a job. *We will have a home, maybe even a kitchen table to eat from*, I imagined.

The image died as the apartment turned into a drug house almost overnight. With people coming and going at all hours, the place was a mess. Most came in, divided the drugs they had just bought, then shot up, and lay around in a dream state until the drug wore off.

"When the heroin ran out, everyone loaded up on barbiturates, which caused terrible rage reactions. They'd fight. Sometimes stabbings or shootings occurred. Finally the police began showing up at the apartment every day."

"Every day?" Donna asked. "What did they do?"

"Just watched the area. Stopped fights. There was one officer I won't forget.

" 'These guys are losers, you do not have to end up like them,' he told me one day.

" 'What do you mean? I'm already like them.'

" 'No, you're not! I can tell this isn't how you want to live. You have more going for you than this. But you've got to decide soon because they will take you down.'

"I just stared at him. He smiled, no judgment in his eyes.

" 'You know, they're not very bright. Watch this,' the officer said, his smile broadening.

"At the apartment door, he knocked, then talked to Tommy, high on barbiturates. Tommy couldn't walk to the door without clutching the wall.

" 'I could take you to jail, you know,' the officer said.

" 'For what?' Tommy slurred loudly.

" 'For being under the influence of drugs.' The officer looked at me and winked.

" 'I'm in my own house. You cannot arrest me in my own house. I am not bothering anyone. Furthermore, how do you know what kind of drugs I am on? I could be taking medicine prescribed by my doctor.' Tommy used his best defense-attorney voice. He learned a lot of law in jail but mostly how to get out of things, not how to abide by it.

" 'I could arrest you for . . .' The officer talked on, taking little backward steps. "Tommy argued his case, belligerent and loose.

"Before Tommy knew it, he was standing on the sidewalk, public territory.

" 'Now I can arrest you, not just for being under narcotics, but disturbing the peace.' Tommy's face was red from shouting his case. Disturbing the peace would be easy to prove.

"The officer looked at me. 'See how stupid they are? Please get away from them. Please take care of yourself.'

" 'I have nowhere to go, no one who cares, no other choices,' I wanted to say, but I couldn't. I looked away.

"The officer patrolled the area often, always checking on me before he left, even if he had to sneak to the back window. 'Are you OK? Please get away from these people. You can do better.'

"Once when he came to the back window, he noticed the electrical box wired with a coat hanger so we could have electricity. The apartment manager had turned off our power weeks ago. The coat hanger turned bright orange and smelled as if it was burning. The officer just removed the coat hanger and left. Soon we moved. I never saw him again. Funny, I missed him. I guess not all officers were cruel.

"The police arrested Tommy again for outstanding warrants, traffic violations, and steep fines. I was desperate. I knew neither he nor I could pay them, so I pleaded with people to help, but when addicts have money, they buy drugs. They don't loan money to 'friends' in need."

I paused.

"What's wrong?" Donna asked, reaching out to touch my arm. "What happened next?"

My face grew hot. *There is no way she will not despise me when I tell her.* "I've never told anyone what happened next. But I want to tell the truth about it." I turned my face in embarrassment." *Can I go on?* I thought.

Donna's warm hand squeezed my shoulder.

"Tommy's ex-girlfriend, Adrian, the mother of one of his children, phoned me.

" 'I will bail Tommy out of jail if you will go away for the weekend. I will only do it if I can spend the weekend with him.'

" 'What? Are you crazy? No.' She had been trying to get him back for a long time. After a while, I knew I'd never raise the money to pay the fines. I needed Tommy back. I felt abandoned.

I swallowed my jealousy.

"I dialed Adrian's number. 'Adrian, are you still interested in getting Tommy out of jail?'

" 'Sure, but the agreement is you'll have to leave town.'

" 'All right. I'll leave.' Adrian, a popular prostitute and drug dealer, had the money. She was the only option.

" 'How will I know you'll stay out of town the whole week-end?'

" 'Come on, don't push it. I will. I promise.' I had nowhere to go.

" 'I have a friend going out of town with a group of friends this weekend. If you go with them, I will bail Tommy out.'

" 'Who are they? Where are they going?' I asked.

" 'Just a group of friends going to Lake Idlewild for the week-end. They are going camping.'

" 'OK.' Camping sounded cool.

" 'Where are you? I'll have someone come by and pick you up,' she said. Was she laughing? I told her where I was and waited for my ride. During the next hour, I brooded over Adrian. The thought of her boiled in me. I loathed her. How often she had tried to yank me from the picture. *Vicious? Yeah, but she'll get Tommy out of jail. Think of that*, I ordered myself.

"*BRRRUMMM.* A sleek Harley Davidson, with gleaming chrome and steel panels revved up on the street in front of me. The bright motor purred hot and clean while the bike's front wheel stretched out in front, at least two feet. My eyes wid-ened. Wow! Then they bulged at the muscled blond riding it, sleek like his bike. The sun-tanned man, perhaps in his early thirties, wore a black leather jacket and stroked his fingers through his tousled hair. *Whoah!* He lifted his dark sunglasses.

" 'Hey. You Cheri?' He shot a friendly grin.

"I nodded, swallowing. I could only stare.

" 'Great. Jump on. This is going to be fun.'

CHAPTER

17

I slid behind him on the seat, slipping my arms around his solid waist, and breathed in the sun-baked leather of his jacket. The wind, too, was warm, filling my lungs and streaming recklessly through my hair. The engine hummed on the gray asphalt, and we rode a long time in silence. My skin tingled, both from fear and excitement. Here, bending around curves, whipping past traffic, feeling the sky and the wind and the strength of this rider, carried fast on the back of a motorcycle going who-knows-where, a heady freedom filled me that I'd never felt before." *This is great!* I reveled.

"We pulled up at an A & W stand for lunch. Walking toward the door, I was able to get a good look at the insignia on the back of his jacket—a Maltese cross with a skull on top and a sword slashed through from top to bottom. Another patch underneath read *Hessians, Southern Cal.* A motorcycle gang! A flickering fear lapped inward from the edges of my thrill, but I quickly doused it. *Come on. He looks really fine and seems nice.* I calmed myself.

" 'My name's Scottie,' my rider told me. "Probably can't tell, but I live for bikes, especially Hogs,' he pointed at his bike. 'I'm going to meet my Bros at a campground for our yearly get-together.'

" 'Why do you meet?' I asked, confident and curious.

" 'For fun and to initiate new members. We drive from all over.'

" 'What do you mean by initiating new members?'

"He changed the subject. 'So have you lived in this area your whole life?' he said, taking a big bite of his hamburger. He pushed a huge order of fries in front of me, asking more questions.

"I ate and ate. I couldn't remember when I'd eaten last. Finishing lunch, we got back on his bike. Scottie fished in his pouch and pulled out some drugs.

" 'Here. Take these,' he said. *Was that an offer or an order? Does it matter?*

"The trip began to drag. Once the drugs kicked in, I slid in and out of consciousness. Sometimes I felt myself slipping off the bike and, struggling, I fought to stay alert. It was a losing battle. Every time I sobered up, Scottie gave me something else to take. For six hours, I clung to the back of his jacket in a twilight mist.

"I jounced awake as Scottie rolled his bike into a beautiful campground, shaded by gigantic trees. The air smelled clean and pungent with pine cones. I'd never been camping before. What fun! My eyes uncrossed and tried to focus. Hundreds of men, women, boys, girls, and even some babies filled my bleary vision. Most, even the children, wore leather or denim jackets. A bikers' convention? Never had I seen so many bikes or bikers in one place, with probably some 300 bikes parked all around.

"I fumbled off the warm seat and stretched my cramping legs. They wobbled. Hearing laughter, I started stumbling over to where the main group was, surrounded by picnic tables stacked with cold kegs of beer.

" 'Get back here. You don't go anywhere unless I say you can go,' Scottie yelled.

" 'What? Are you talking to me?' I turned, stunned. *Does he feel he has the right to tell me what I can or cannot do? I will stay here for the weekend, but I am not his girlfriend or anything.* I snapped. 'I can go anywhere I want, you old . . .' " I stopped for respect to Donna.

"The next thing I knew, a kick smashed me on the ground underneath a small pine, shockwaves of pain pounding my back.

"Who does he think he is? He'll never get away with hitting me again. Fury rose. I had to defend myself, from him, from everything. Struggling up with help from a tree, I swung my fist as hard as I could, hitting Scottie on the rough of his chin. The whole campground seemed to freeze, and even eyes on the far side of the camp bored into me.

" 'Scottie, are you going to let that . . . get away with that?'

"Obscenities soured thick. Scottie's fist rammed into my face, the blow slamming me back into the tree. I slid down the trunk of the tree and lay crumpled on the pine needles. My ears buzzed, and I couldn't focus. Though my whole body cried to stay there, I couldn't. All the injustice I had ever faced up to this very minute flashed bright red before my eyes. I wouldn't take it.

"I pulled myself up, inching. I whaled with all my might at Scottie's face. He laughed and swatted my fist aside. He smashed me again, back under the tree. Lying there, I tasted blood in my mouth. *Where is it coming from?* Now no pain, only rage, blotted all light from my sky.

People's laughter surrounded me, but all sounds seemed far away. I got up, this time more slowly. I lunged at him with both fists, pounding. The world turned purple as I heard him laughing louder.

"Suddenly he stopped, grabbed me by the neck, lifted me slightly off the ground, and struck me full in the face. I heard a voice, mine, cry out when I hit the tree the third time. This time I slid to the ground and stayed. *Come on. Get up.* I yelled from within, but couldn't move. My muscles twitched in vain.

" 'Just stay down,' Scottie's voice warned. Somewhere men were joking and laughing at 'that gutsy broad.' My eyes fuzzed red.

" 'I'll teach you how to be my old lady. I admire you. You'll make a good one.'

The way this group looked at things amazed me. I never have wanted to hurt someone as badly as I wished to hurt him. I would have killed him if could. And now, after all that, I had gained the admiration and respect of this perverse group. My mind went black.

"When I came to, my body was screaming in pain. I cautiously propped myself up to a sitting position, my head resting on the trunk where I had fallen. I touched my face. Ouch. It hurt everywhere. Cuts on my lip and one on my right cheek stung, and my nose felt out of shape. Could my cheekbone and nose be broken? My face was puffy, and huge lumps clumped all over the back of my head. My eyes were swollen too.

" 'Are you all right?' Scottie bent over me, his voice friendly and casual. 'I hope you'll feel better soon. From this point on, it would be wise to just listen and obey me, OK?'

" 'OK.' It took everything in me to say it. 'Do you have something to kill the pain?'

"Resting quietly for a while, I heard a wail of terror. A girl's cry. Where was it coming from? Across the camp a group of men and women held down a struggling young girl. When my blurring eyes focused, I gasped. She was my age or younger. Her long blond hair was tangled with dirt and debris from the ground and her ripped clothes hung loose from her thin arms and legs. 'Let me go,' she begged, crying. A fat, dirty man cuffed her in the face and raped her.

" 'Scottie!' I screamed hoarsely. 'Help her. Somebody. Stop

them!' The group was laughing.

" 'Shut up and mind your own business.' He smiled.

" 'Scottie, you've got to do something!' More people were pulled into the rape scene. It was a nightmare. 'Scottie, please. We can't just let this happen. Save her! Come on!'

"Scottie grabbed my face, his breath hot and violent, and pulled me inches from his.

" 'If you want to take her place, go ahead. If you don't, then shut up. Do not say another word about her. Don't even look over in that direction.' He pushed me away.

"Sober as death, I hurt for her, biting my tongue. By this time, people were all over her. I couldn't stand it. 'You have to help her, please.'

"Scottie jumped up, kicked me in the side and chest as I fell. Then gripping my hair, he dragged me through the trees to a secluded spot. My skin ripping, I tried to hold onto his hand to lessen the pain from my head, but I couldn't.

" 'If you do not shut up, you could end up dead. I can't believe how stupid you are. For the rest of the weekend, you will stay right here,' he yelled. Throwing me on the ground, he stalked back toward camp.

"Why didn't I run? I've since asked myself. I could hear laughter and jokes floating from the camp. Now and then I could hear the little girl, and then another girl's cry joined hers. So this was the initiation. I lay sobbing until I fell asleep.

"I jerked awake to a man rubbing my back. It was dark.

" 'Scottie said I could have sex with you.'

" 'What?' I shrank in horror.

" 'Well, tell Scottie I said No!' I shut my eyes, sick. A wind gust chilled me.

"Ten minutes later, Scottie walked up and kicked me in the chest. He stood over me, completely naked, a silver glint of a gun in his hand, from a lifeless moonlight. Though his face was masked by night, I sensed his snarled lips.

" 'When I tell someone they can have sex with you, they can have sex with you!' "

" 'No.'

"He grabbed me by the hair, striking me with the gun, then pressing it hard against my head.

" 'You are my property. I could kill you, and no one would care. You are nothing. Did you hear me? This is the order of things here. Number one, my bikes; two, my Bros; and last, my old ladies. You're mine. You have no voice here and no opinions. You will be taught to be part of this group."

" 'No.' I whispered, shaking. *Go ahead. Kill me.* My body hurt, but that was not the reason. *I'm done being abused, especially sexually*. I shut my eyes and waited.

"Scottie stepped away. I cracked open my eyes.

" 'Do you like games? I do. Let's play.' He flipped bullets from the gun.

"Ripping my pants, he shook me like a rag doll, yelling. My mind switched off.

"I've learned early in life to disassociate when things get too bizarre or hurtful. I go somewhere else in my mind, somewhere safe. Scottie seemed to know, because he grabbed my face until I refocused, demanding my involvement.

" 'Do you know Russian Roulette?' He took all the bullets from the gun except one. Grabbing a leg, he pulled my feet out from under me and shoved the gun inside me.

" 'Are you going to? Or will I have to pull the trigger?'

"I just stared at him.

"Click.

"My mind divorced itself from me. I remembered little more.

" 'What do you want me to do, Rob? Kill her?' Scottie seemed to be talking to the president of the local chapter of Hessians. I heard their footsteps crunching away through the night, their laughter leaving a residue of filth behind them. 'She is tough.'

"I disassociated again. I learned when I'm being violated not to think about the abuse. What good does it do? I can't change anything. By disassociating, I could flee the pain, both emotional and physical. But the physical pain was nothing next to the emotional pain. It never was."

"I cannot imagine how you must have felt," Donna said, leaning over and holding my hand.

"I doubt if I've ever let myself feel the full impact of that assault."

Donna opened her mouth to say something, but she hesitated.

"Just say it."

"When you talk about all the terrible abuse that biker did to you, abuse that would forever change someone and maybe even kill them, you speak as if you are telling about an unpleasant trip you took—one you would not recommend, but nothing more. Do you hear me?"

I drank her eyes in deeply, eyes full of concern and sadness. Tears seeped into my eyes. "It must be drug withdrawal," I sniffed.

"I've taught myself not to feel, not to think, and not to show any reaction to abuse around me. It's always been this way. The only reasons I wasn't raped and possibly killed is because of the defenses I learned so well. If I would have cried and pleaded with those guys, I wouldn't have gotten the respect I did. With them, if you can give or take abuse, you're respected. That respect kept me from experiencing even greater violation. And, yes, I do know that this brutal, evil encounter with these people has changed my life forever. I can no longer see people as safe or basically good. No more illusion of safety. What little innocence and naiveté left in my already shredded soul was gone. Only a hole was left."

"How did you get away from them?" Donna asked.

CHAPTER

18

Scottie came back later that same night.

" 'We're leaving. If I don't get you out of here, you're going to get yourself killed. Once we return to LA, we will teach you the things you need to know to stay alive.'

"I helped him pack. He was high on acid, so it was hard for him to focus. Eventually, things were secured onto the bike, and we rode out of camp. He gave me more drugs, which I swallowed gladly; they would help me to escape, somewhat. But the pain! Every bump and pebble in the road jolted and jarred my body.

"It must have been three or four in the morning when Scottie pulled off the main road into a family campground.

" 'This is a family campground,' I argued. When a Harley pulls up beside you in the middle of nowhere, it tends to wake you up. 'Have you seen my face? Have you seen yourself? We can't stay here!'

" 'Naw.' Scottie scoffed, high and rude. 'They need their education, too, just like you.' "As Scottie and I unloaded the sleeping bags and guns, the family next to us, nervously, without drawing too much attention to themselves, were packing up their kids and leaving. " 'This is education!' Scottie yelled at them among curses. They packed faster. I was in danger, too, but it did me no good to think. I just needed to be alert to react if I had to, to be safe.

"The next day we got up, packed, and rode back to Long Beach. Scottie took me to his house, introducing me to his 'old lady,' his girlfriend Linda. She would educate me, and I was to listen, follow directions, not ask questions, and not talk back. She wasn't thrilled about having me in her house, but she seemed used to it.

"The next day Scottie left early, leaving me with Linda. For the three days he was gone, I rested. Linda supplied me with an incredible amount of drugs to ease the pain. During times I was rational, I tried to help with the housework, but she wasn't talkative. Not to me. There were always many bikers around the house, so I just stayed out of the way, not wanting to be noticed.

" 'We're going out,' Scottie said when he got back. 'Help get her dressed. She looks like . . .' He rarely talked directly to me when Linda was around. Irritated, she gave me some of her clothes to wear.

"We pulled into a dingy bar in Long Beach, the parking lot full of motorcycles. Groups of people, laughing and high, hung out among the bikes. They could hurt, if not kill, me without a second thought I squinted in the bright light. I had no doubt. *Is this part of my learning process?* I groaned. Scottie led us inside, told me to sit in back by the pool table, and left with Linda.

I sat there staring at the green felt of the table, listening to the click-click of the pool balls as some guys played.

"At least fifty bikers and their 'old ladies' loitered around me. I sat there, not trying to escape, watching everything. *Scottie will kill me before this ordeal is over. There's no way out.*

"Then the atmosphere changed. People scurried around hiding things, whispering, and cleaning up.

" 'What's going on?' I asked. Scottie was in front of me, pushing a gun into my hands.

'No.' I had never held one.

" 'Hide it,' he ordered. I took the gun, my hands trembling, and put it in the back of my pants. I sat there shaking.

"The front door opened, and the police walked in. The police! *Oh no. I have a gun on me! What was it used for? Was it wanted in a crime?* I was afraid of the bikers. And I was afraid of the police.

"Rob, the president of the gang, grabbed my arm. 'Come with me, quick!'

"I yanked away. *Where did he come from?* The last time I had seen him was at the campground, standing near while Scottie played Russian roulette. 'Get lost.'

" 'It's OK. Follow me.'

"I got up and quickly followed him outside through a back door to a parking lot behind. 'Do you have the gun?' he asked. How did he know I had it? I nodded.

" 'Good. Just follow me over to the car. When we get into the car, put the gun in the glove box.' He was still giving me instructions when we heard footsteps coming around the corner.

" 'It's the police! Act like we are making out.'

"*No!* He pulled me to him and kissed me. My mind spun. What am I doing here. Aghh! The police are coming around the corner, and I still have this gun in my pants.

"An officer, I thought, grabbed me by the back of my hair and slammed me into a parked car behind me. Then I heard Scottie shouting.

" 'When I gave you permission to be with this guy, you said No, but now I find you with him in the parking lot. I am finished with you. You have no identity. You are nothing. From now on, you belong to the group.'

" 'Go get some beer,' Scottie told the guys standing near. 'We are going to turn her out.'

No!

"He bashed me in the head, then my chest. I couldn't breathe, and blood rushed to my mouth." *I must be badly hurt.* 'Linda, bring her over to BJ's house.' I knew BJ was the national president of the gang, but I hadn't been to his house before. I fainted on the way there.

" 'Here, you are going to need these.' Linda bent over me with a handful of pills, her face triumphant. *She's glad they're going to rape me. I'm finally out of her hair.* Angry, I took the pills I knew I needed to be totally out of it. My mind flooded with brutal pictures of the two girls at the campground, raped, urinated on, and beaten. Tonight I would be the prey.

"The drugs kicked in, pulling me into a dark, safe corner of my mind. *Bam.* A slap on the face jarred me. A tall man with long sandy blond hair, wearing the same jean jacket everyone else had, stood over me.

" 'From now on you will take orders from me. Get up.'

"Sitting on the floor, I tried to stand, but I couldn't. I had taken too many barbiturates. " 'No. You will be sorry if you touch me,' I slurred. 'You don't know who you're messing with.'

" 'Shut up!' He hit me again. 'You will take orders from me or anyone else here tonight. You will serve them. If they want a beer, something to eat, or a piece of you, get it for them. Do you understand?' He grabbed me by my clothes and pulled me up.

"He turned to Linda. "She's wasted. Get her some uppers. That will bring her out.'

"Linda returned with a handful of whites, amphetamines and stimulants. She thrust them in my face.

" 'Take them,' BJ said.

"I stared at them through blurred vision. *No, I will save*

them. I knew what the night would bring. I did not want to be awake for it. I reached for a pack of cigarettes, pulled the cellophane off the package, poured the pills into the wrapping, and placed them carefully in my bra for later.

"The room had grown intensely quiet.

"BJ kicked me in the face. 'Everyone, get out of here,' he yelled.

"I moaned on the floor as people gathered up their things and left.

Donna sighed. Compassion glowed in her eyes. But where was the judgment? After all, how could I be so stupid? I kept getting myself into messes. How could she stand it? But I didn't want to be messed up. I didn't want to be a drug addict. I just wanted to be safe and to be loved. Could she see that? A strange feeling startled me again. I couldn't shake it off. *Is this love?*

CHAPTER

19

Donna, can we take another walk? I'm overwhelmed even talking about those two weeks. The pictures are too vivid. I'm scared."

Donna stood and reached out her hand to pull me out of my chair. But even more, her acceptance and love was a warm grip helping me up, out of my past. She couldn't fully know.

The shadows haunted the edges of the pines now as we walked along the trail. *What was that? Was someone behind that tree?* I knew a biker would jump out from behind it to tear me into pieces. The forest that just hours before had made me breathe deeply and enjoy, now filled me with fright. My breath was short and shallow.

Walking over to a fallen tree, I sat down on the sagging bark, lost in thought. *God, please make Yourself real to me. I need to know that You are here. I need to be safe, for once. I want so much to know that You are real, that You love me.*

How can You really love me with this garbage of my life? And how can I ever be normal? I don't even know how to act in any situation, unless I am drugged. I have nothing of value that I do or that I know. I have only done what I thought those around me expected of me my whole life in order to survive. God, I am worthless . . .

A beautiful bluebird fluttered to a branch within a few feet of where I sat. The thin branch quivered and bounced as she ruffled her feathers, beginning to preen. I could have touched her. *Why isn't she afraid of me?*

The answer landed, as quick and as soft as the bird, in my heart. She was not afraid because God took care of her. God would keep her safe.

"And I'll keep you safe, too, Cheri."

He'll keep me safe.

A burst of joy filled me, and I wanted to leap from the trunk and whoop, but the bird was still there. I didn't want to scare it. *Was this voice that I heard silly? No.* I was too afraid to ask Donna, but I knew it was real.

I breathed the forest air deep, filling every possible space in my lungs. The air was fresh and the shadows but playful. The forest was beautiful again. The bird stretched its wings.

Goodbye. Thank you! In a blue swoop of feathers and cheer, the bird was gone. *Does God use nature to teach us about Him?* I wondered. *Of course He does! He just did.*

"God has given us so much, and all we have to do is accept it," Donna said, almost to herself. She sat on a large lichen-covered stone, breathing in the beauty too.

Looking around at the dancing green boughs and the whispering grass, I agreed. If I couldn't accept it officially, my heart knew how. An inner warmth lifted me. *I am safe!*

"Can I tell you what happened next?" We continued our hike.

"Yes. How did you ever get away from them?"

"That night ended in a blur, and I passed out. The next thing I knew, it was daytime, and everyone was gone. Everyone except for BJ and Linda. Opening my eyes, I lay on the floor and listened to their chatter. *Am I safe or not?* Usually, I figured it out quickly, but now I was confused.

" 'Good morning, sunshine.' BJ, the guy with sandy hair, said when he saw my eyes open. Strange, he didn't mention the night before, other than to joke about me putting the pills in the cigarette wrapper and down my bra. 'You're really gutsy.'

" 'You'll be living here. If you need anything, ask Linda. I will make sure no one hurts you. You'll no longer answer to Scottie, only to me. I'll teach you how to act so you don't get killed.' I seemed like an invited guest.

"Listening for a while, I knew I had to play this out or I would never make it out alive. I smiled when he smiled, nodded at the appropriate times, even laughed at a poor joke. While I saw no bars on the windows or armed guards blocking the doors, the prison was real. I'd have to be very careful about planning my escape for, if caught, it was all over. Favor wouldn't grace me again.

"The next few days I was a puppet doing whatever I was told, and with enthusiasm. I acted as if I really liked BJ. Whenever other guys were around, I stayed close to him. No one challenged his authority. No one except Linda. She huffed and glared at me, her jaw clamped. Who she belonged to now I couldn't tell, but she liked BJ, and she hated me. " 'I miss my boyfriend,' I mentioned one morning when we were alone together.

" 'You have a boyfriend?' That was all it took. 'You want to go back to him?' "

" 'I wish I could.'

" 'We can work something out,' she said, now friendly. 'I'll help you plan your escape.'

" 'But you'll be beaten for letting me run away.'

" 'So, I'll deal with it.' I stared at her, incredulous. She had her reasons.

"Buried hope scratched to the surface. I was a threat, and she wanted me gone. As for me, I had no interest in her life or taking her place. I detested being a biker. Since I was often left with Linda to watch over me, we waited. One morning, all the bikers left. We chatted uneasily.

" 'Quick. Get up and get out!' Linda whispered, after fifteen minutes had passed. 'Here's your chance. Hurry!'

"Gratefulness squeezed my fear in two. I smiled, gulped, and slipped out the door."

"Whew!" Donna said. "Did you go back to Tommy? Was he now out of jail?"

"Yes. I found my way back and went into hiding for a while."

"Were you scared they would chase you?"

"Oh, I had the worst nightmares ever, even if I soused myself with drugs. The dreams were always the same. Scottie would lunge from behind, grab my hair, and throw me down. Suddenly, hundreds of bikers swarmed around me, all filthy, drunk, and leering. They dragged me across a field toward a large group of savages. I would wake screaming, knowing what would happen next. But I ground all my feelings to pulp in my mind, ignoring them. I had to survive.

" 'You idiot!' Tommy yelled when he heard what happened. While he was livid at Adrian, he scorned me for being so stupid. 'When you're on the street, you have to be smart to survive. I could sell ice cubes in Alaska, but you . . . what a fool!' Well, if he spurned me or not, at least I was safer with him, if he could only stay out of jail. He couldn't. Soon he was arrested for possession of stolen goods, and since he was on probation, he'd be in jail a long time. Again I was on my own.

"I called home, not really knowing why. 'Cheri?' My younger sister, Becky, answered the phone. 'Where are you? Thank God. Can I come stay with you?'

" 'What?' I asked, taken aback. 'What happened to your husband?' She was only fifteen.

" 'I left him. When we split up, I was so mad I slammed my

fist through a glass door and slashed up my arm pretty deep. It took them more than two hours to stitch it up. It's trying to heal, but I'm a mess. Cheri, I can't stay home in this pit. I don't know what to do or where to go. I'll be out on the streets. I need time to heal. Please, can I come stay with you?'

"But I'm on the streets myself. She has no clue what my life is like. 'Sure,' I said, eager. It would be good to be near family who wanted me. *She needs a quiet place, and I need her. But where will we stay?*

"I twisted out a loan from the owner of the club I worked at to rent an apartment. Becky moved in with me. It was sparse, but it was ours. She mustn't see what life is really like on the street, that I do drugs, I worried. Sometimes, she'd catch a glimpse, but I guarded it from her, just trying to give her a good time. We partied constantly, always had people over, or had places to go.

"One day the door of the apartment opened. Becky was back early. Sitting on the floor with my arm tied off with a rubber tunic and a needle sticking into my veins, I frantically pulled the needle out and tried to hide everything, but I wasn't fast enough."

'What are you doing?' she screamed. 'Is that what I think it is? You're doing heroin! How long have you been doing heroin? You have to stop it!'

" 'Come on, it's OK. It's not that big of a deal.' She kept on yelling, not hearing one word. 'Give me that.' She yanked the needle out of my hand and smashed it on the carpet, breaking the tip.

" 'Hey, what are you doing?'

"She grabbed the bag of heroin and ran into the bathroom.

" 'Becky, No! That is not mine. I am selling that for some- one.' She dumped the powder into the bowl. 'Do you know how much that costs?' By the time she heard me, the heroin was dissolving in the toilet, with no way to save it. And no way to save our relationship. I had lost her respect.

"I had to work extra shifts to make up the money to pay off the supplier. Becky also started working in the clubs. I hated to see her there, getting exposed to some pretty sick people, but I knew no other options to give her, and the money was good.

"I loved the time we spent together, but Becky was much more social. I was not always welcome with her new friends. She spent a lot of time with the club owners and people with money. I didn't feel I belonged with them.

"One night as we were working, my ex-husband Wayne came into the club. I hadn't seen him since he took off with the navy.

" 'What are you doing now?' I asked.

" 'Driving trucks. I'm taking a load to New York now. Hey, want to come with me?'

" 'Sure. Let me go tell my sister where I am going, and I'll be back,' I said, excited and ready for adventure.

" 'Wayne just showed up. Remember him? He's going to New York, and I'm going with him.'

" 'What?'

" 'I will be back in a few days.'

" 'I want to go too,' she said, laughing.

"We walked into the office. 'We're off to New York,' we told the manager.

" 'If you leave before the end of your shift, you're fired,' the manager said, trying to sound serious.

" 'We quit. See you when we get back.' We both ran out, laughing like a couple of kids.

" 'Be careful,' the manager called. We all knew he wouldn't fire us. We were young and good for business.

"The trip to New York was uneventful, except that Wayne had a partner who drove with him. This partner became extremely infatuated with Becky. While at first this bothered her, after a while she realized that he would pay for all her meals, cigarettes, and even buy her little gifts at truck stops.

" 'Let's stop here!' We begged, riding along in the cab. The miles stretched out endlessly.

" 'Nope. I've got a deadline. We don't have time to stop. I have to have this load in New York in three days. Here,' Wayne said, opening a pouch full of drugs. 'Take a trip with these.'

" 'Oh, yeah!' sang Becky. She popped one in her mouth. 'What will these do?' She'd come a long way since the heroin incident. Staying high, the trip flew fast.

" 'Welcome to New York,' I read as the truck sped into the state. 'Get ready to party!' " " 'We're only staying one night here and then heading back.' Wayne said. When we arrived at his destination, he rented a motel room for the night. Becky and I jumped out, wobbly-legged and sore. We'd been stuck in the truck for days.

" 'What? Come on,' Becky whined. 'We just got here. Let's have some fun. I heard about this really hip after-hour club in this city. Let's go.' In the motel, I showered and started getting ready for the night when I heard Becky yell from outside.

" 'I don't care what you say. You have no say in what I do or where I go,' her voice was fire. *Who is she talking to?* It wasn't Wayne. Quickly dressing, I opened the door. 'If you ever hit me again, you are dead. Do you hear me?' She was talking to Wayne's partner up in the cab. Becky threw our small bundles out of the cab onto the ground. She then stepped off the truck, forgetting the height, and fell clumsily to the ground.

" 'We're out of here. Don't try to follow us, or I'll call the police.' She brushed her hands on her jeans, looked up, and saw me, her face purple like rhubarb.

" 'I'm walking home. Are you coming?' "

CHAPTER

20

W hat? You're walking home? Do you realize we are in New York? Home is in California. That's 3,000 miles away.' Becky stalked down the street. 'Wait up.' Awkwardly, I clopped behind in my platform shoes, trying to catch up.

" 'Let's get a soda and plan our next move,' I said, seeing a truck stop with a small place to eat. I laughed. I had no clue how we'd get home, but this was adventure. Becky was funny, and I loved being with her. Will this be safe? The ever-present question loomed. Now I had my little sister to look after too. 'I guess we're walking home. I have to keep you safe,' I told her.

" 'That's a joke,' Becky snickered. 'I'm more cautious than you are.'

" 'Whatever.' She was right. The first thing she did was buy a map and chart our return trip. I would have winged it. Drinking our sodas, we sat at the table discussing our plight. 'How are we going to do this,' I asked.

" 'Hitchhike.' Two men at the table beside us watched us.

" 'You two girls are in luck. We are going to Ventura, Cali-

The Cheri Peters Story

fornia. Wanna ride?' One of the men leaned over.

" 'Yeah!' I said, shocked, bursting into a smile. I gave Becky a high five.

"At first, everything was fun. The driver I rode with was funny, asked questions, and made jokes. Suddenly, his comments started getting crude, the jokes sexual. I squirmed.

" 'I'll teach you to be my driving partner.' One man winked.

" 'Don't you want to be a 'truck-driving mama?' Becky teased me during stops, when I told her I was feeling creepy.

" 'My dream come true,' I laughed. The guy would hold my hand for long headlight-beaming miles, singing country love songs. When his voice tired, he picked up a coffee cup and sang into it. It helped amplify his voice, he said.

"Though they were obnoxious, we could handle this. We'd be home in a few days. "We drove into Ohio early the next morning. Propped up against one driver in the small cab, I struggled to keep awake. I've got to stay awake. I don't trust these guys. Becky may need me. I dozed. Becky was riding with the other driver in his cab.

"Pull over!" Becky's driver shouted to mine, popping his head out the cab window. He slammed on his brakes. It was raining hard, and the wheels steamed black skids over the wet asphalt. " 'You either give it up or get out. It is up to you.' Becky's driver yelled at her. *Oh no!*

"Rustling dark cornfields surrounded us, cornfields for miles. They wouldn't throw us out here, would they?

" 'It's not as if you've never given it up before,' I poked at Becky as we watched the trucks hiss away. We both laughed and started sloshing down the soggy highway.

"Hitchhiking down the road, most offers made were from men wanting sex in exchange for a lift. When they figured out it wasn't going to happen, they dropped us off.

"One guy who seemed really concerned picked us up. *Yeah, right*, I thought. Becky and I had just eaten before he stopped.

" 'Are you two hungry?'

" 'No,' I said, sounding pitiful as if I was hungry but didn't want to bother him. " 'She's just playing around. We're not hungry, really. We just ate,' Becky said.

" 'I don't believe you. We're pulling over.'" 'No, I really was teasing.' I tried to convince him. He insisted, so Becky and I ate for the second time in less than an hour. We were stuffed.

" 'Sorry, but I can only take you girls about 100 miles,' he told us. In the back of his big rig he had a small bed. Exhausted, Becky and I decided to sleep in shifts so we could make sure we stayed to the map. Becky slept first.

"The truck driver seemed nice. 'I can take you 50 miles further if we take another road,' he said. Finding the road on the map, it headed in the right direction." 'OK,' I agreed. Becky wouldn't know.

"The road was two lanes and not well traveled. *This doesn't look right.* Then a tree branch scraped the top of the truck as we drove by, waking Becky up.

" 'Where are we?" she demanded, grabbing the map.

" 'Well, we took a shortcut,'I reassured her.

" 'Trees would not be hitting the top of this truck if other trucks traveled here.'

"*She's right. My heart beat quicker.*

" 'Turn around now, or pull over and let us out,' Becky shouted, scared.

" 'Relax.You're safe. I promise I'll take you to your destination. This isn't a well-traveled road, but I'm just trying to help you out and take you farther.'" 'I bet: how much farther?' screeched Becky. 'Let us out now!'

" 'I promise I'll drop you off without any funny business. But not here.There aren't many cars on this road, and you will be stranded.' We calmed and eventually could talk to him. He was very pleasant, no sexual jokes or propositions. Every once in a while, a tree scraped the top of the truck.

" 'I'm going in another direction here,' he finally said, pulling off the road onto a bigger highway. 'Here's goodbye. Are you two tired?' Were we ever!

"Becky and I looked at each other, then at him. *Here it goes. He is going to try something.*

" 'No, listen,' he said, his forehead crinkling. 'I will pay for a room for one night so you can get some sleep and clean up before heading out on the rest of your journey. I am not staying. I am not coming on to you!' We stared at him, shocked.

"He did just what he said. Renting a motel room for us, he gave us some money for dinner and left. Thank you for being good, I wanted to say, but couldn't. With no strings attached, the guy disappeared down the road. I will never forget him.

" 'Hey, Becky,' I said the next morning, looking at the map. 'We're close to Bethany, Oklahoma. That's where Grandma and Grandpa live, Dad's parents.'

'Really?' Becky's eyes brightened. 'Wow!' We called information.

" 'Hello, Grandma?' I said, after finding their number. By the sound of her voice, she was disappointed to hear from me, but I didn't tell Becky. She had never met them. She thought they loved us like regular grandparents loved their grandchildren. I knew better. They gave us directions to their house.

"It took two rides to get there. One of the rides started out fine, but soon the familiar unsafe feeling oozed in. Another creep. Asking to go to the bathroom, we went in, waited, and then climbed out the bathroom window to the bushes. The next ride we hitched took us right to their door.

"Tap. Tap. The door opened. Becky and I stood bedraggled and worn out in our eight-inch high platform shoes, our faces thick with red lipstick, blush, and heavy eye shadow.

" 'You're just passing through, right?' my grandma asked, faking a smile.

" 'Yes, yes. We're not staying. We just needed help getting

home.' *Relax, you old hag*, I muttered inside. *Don't let Becky down.*

"Lying in a makeshift bed in the extra bedroom that night, I heard arguing. 'We will not be responsible for them,' my grandma said on the phone. Who was she talking to? 'Well, we aren't going to pay for them to get home,' her voice was ice.

"After two days, my grandparents finally got the money from my dad to send us home.

" 'We can manage on our own,' I told them. Their conscience wouldn't let us just walk out. Their conscience, not affection, kept them from asking us to leave. Finally, we were given bus tickets from Oklahoma to California. The trip was long, but we were safe.

" 'Next time you decide to walk home, check with me first.' We laughed.

"Arriving at our apartment, we opened our eviction notice. With loud parties all the time and drug selling, it was no surprise but awful timing.

" 'Come stay with me in Hollywood,' Becky offered. She was moving in with a girlfriend. I stayed with her a while, but I didn't fit in with her friends, so I left. Sadness throbbed in me like an aching tooth. For the first time I had felt connected, not so lost."

Donna and I were approaching the house, returning from our hike. "Do you still see her now?"

"Not much. I miss her. It has never been the same since then. When we do get together, we tell stories and laugh, but it's different." I appreciated her for asking. *She seems to understand.*

Walking into the house, I heard laughter bubbling from the living room. Inside, the family was still sitting around, telling stories, joking with each other, and laughing. *This is exactly what a home should be like. It feels so warm. The people here are safe and care about each other. They enjoy each other's company. Will I ever have this? Of course not.* My face felt plastic and . . .

A streak of blue swooped across my mind. I remembered the bluebird and smiled.

CHAPTER 21

"Continue your story," Donna said, eager to hear. The next morning we went outside to the back porch to talk. "You moved to Hollywood with your sister, but you didn't live with her long. What was Hollywood like?"

"Weird, but for the most part, it's like anywhere else. My sister and her friend rented an apartment in a rundown building, once Hollywood finery. An elevator with iron gates had to be manually closed to run. *Just like the movies*, I thought. The apartment was one small living room with a huge double-doored closet. At night, a bed was pulled down from the wall, turning the room into a bedroom.

"The last night I spent there, I got ready for work at the club, packed up my things, fed our new little puppy, and walked into the bathroom to finish my hair and makeup. Just as I opened my steam curlers, the dog ran under my feet, tripping me. Whacking the curling set off the counter, I spilled scorching water down my leg."

"Ouch!" Donna winced.

A Miracle from the Streets

"My skin melted, then swelled up into a purple bubble. I ran to the fridge for ice. None. Butter? Nope. Pain shot up my leg. I needed something now. But where to go? I knocked on the neighbor's door to borrow some ice or butter. Through the door I heard voices, but no one answered. I knocked harder. It got super quiet, with people scurrying around, whispering.

"The door creaked open two inches. An eye squinted at me.

" 'What do you want?'

" 'I'm your next-door neighbor. I just moved in. I am sorry to bother you, but I burned my leg. Do you have any ice or butter? It's burned bad." I rushed, trying to get the story out before the door might shut.

" 'You need what?' he asked, annoyed. 'We're in the middle of a shoot.'

" 'What does she want.' I heard someone in the background curse.

" 'I think she wants some butter,' one laughed.

" 'Want some oil? We've got plenty.' More laughter.

" 'OK. Wait here,' the man at the door said. 'I will get you some ice and butter.'

"As he walked away, the door creaked open a few more inches. A studio with a huge bed in the middle of it was flooded with lights and covered with slimy nudes, oozing oil. My mouth gaped. So this is Hollywood. Ice and butter waved in my face. Click. The door shut. I left to doctor my wounds.

"Leaving my sister's apartment, I was on my own again. Though my loss of companionship cut keenly, I couldn't stay with her. Struggling to fit in with her crowd was worse than the loneliness without her. The world I saw was sick, abusive, and morally bankrupt. No one anywhere seemed good. Survival was my best hope; I tried to avoid being hurt. I couldn't think about life, only react to it, keeping safe."

"Where did you go next?" Donna asked.

"I floated from place to place until I met Don. He was nice, quiet, and he liked me. 'I want to take care of you,' he told me. We spent more and more time together."

"What was Don like?"

"He was a Vietnam vet and rather strange. He loved showing off his scars and talking about Vietnam. When I saw his scars, I gasped. His entire body was covered with thick and nasty-looking welts. Had someone fired a machine gun at him, or had a hand grenade blown up in his face? Don would never say. Joking around, he changed the story every time.

" 'Please tell me what happened to you,' I begged one day.

" 'Well . . . OK. I was attacked one day while walking alone out in the jungle. . . .' He laughed.

" 'By whom?

" 'By a swarm of huge bumblebees!'

" 'No way!'

" 'Yep. Can you believe it? It's embarrassing to tell. Other vets have these horrible war stories, and me, I just had bumblebees. Won't tell, will you?'

" 'No,' I said, still laughing. The attack wasn't funny. It must have been terrifying, and he almost died. But it's not a riveting war story.

"I moved in with Don, and my memory turns to mush. We did drugs and partied with his friends. He actually had a job and didn't live on the streets or run with the same people I knew. Getting a normal job, I worked in a factory running a punch press. I did OK, I guess, except for one thing. The factory owners had us tape tongue depressors on our fingertips because there were no safety doors to keep hands away from the press. If I didn't get my hands out in time, the machine would hack off the depressor, not my fingers.

" "That's positive," Donna cringed. "You still have your fingers, but what happened?"

"Well, I got too many tongue depressors cut off. I was fired."

"Did you stay long with Don?"

"He asked me to marry him. What marriage or commitment was, I had no clue. Sure, I'd been married a couple years ago at thirteen, but no big deal. Why not? With him I would be safe and finally have a home. Would he leave me? I didn't think about it. When I went home and told my family, they loved it and got involved right away planning the wedding. I loved the attention and time I got with my mom and step-father and even grandparents."

"How old were you?"

"Fifteen. Don and I decided to wait until I was sixteen to get married. My parents didn't care, and Don's mom was getting used to the idea. She hated that Don at twenty-four was marrying me, but she'd given up trying to talk him out of it."

"How was the wedding?"

"Beautiful. I wore a white wedding dress. It was so exciting. Don looked handsome in his tuxedo. My whole family played a part in the ceremony. It was wonderful." I sighed. "We got married in a Baptist church, had the reception over at my grandmother's house, then went home to play house.

" 'We have to make a clean break,' Don said soon after the wedding. 'We've got to get away from family, friends, and especially drugs, all our bad influences. I've decided we're moving to Santa Barbara.'

" 'You've decided? You're kidding. I'll never go there! I won't go.'

" 'You will.'

"We moved to Santa Barbara with me kicking and screaming all the way."

"Did he clean up as he said?"

"Once we moved there, Don was gone all the time. 'Bowling,' he said. 'I want to be a professional bowler, so I've got to practice.'

" 'Seven nights a week?' I retorted. He ignored me.

"All day, every day, I sat in our one-bedroom apartment. We

had no money, and what money Don made went to bowling. The only time I saw him was at night when he was drunk, demanding sex. 'You are mine.' I left one day with just the clothes I was wearing and headed back to Los Angeles."

"Where did you go?" Donna asked.

"Tommy was back. He'd been out of jail for a few months. I went back to what I knew.

" 'You've gotten married? You're kidding,' he yelled when I told him.

" 'I don't believe it either.'

" 'I thought you loved me.'

" 'I never even asked myself that.'

" 'Well start asking. Did you love him?"

" 'I don't know. All I know is that he liked me, at first, anyway. Hey, it was fun to have my family so involved with me and my life.'

"Tommy spit. 'Whatever. Well, you'll only be safe with me. Never forget that.' Tommy's words haunted me. *Do I believe that? I must, because I always run back to him.* I was back to doing heroin, a lot, staying high every day. And I was back with my 'family' who cared. Here I could belong. I mattered to them. Strange, I did feel safe again. Until one night.

"At the drug house where we stayed, there was a huge party, some people I knew and some I didn't. Tommy had just received a shipment of Mexican heroin, and the place was buzzing with the buying, selling, and weighing of drugs. A black guy staggered in, his face puffy, his bloodshot eyes rolling back in his head. Too many drugs. He slammed into a wall, bounced back and knocked the table, sending neat piles of heroin crumbling.

" 'I don't feel well,' he said.

" 'Shut up and lie down.' they yelled, fixing the piles and dividing more heroin. Some things were more important.

"I jolted awake from thick sleep at 3:00 a.m., my head foggy and underwater slow.

" 'He's dead," someone said. 'The black guy was found dead in the bedroom.'

" 'Yuck. What happened?' someone else replied.

"I listened, stunned.

" 'He must have overdosed or something. Who was he?' a girl asked.

" 'Don't know. We just took him to the hospital and dropped him off,' another said.

" 'What did the doctors say?'

" 'You think we'd go in? They'd have jumped on us. We just dropped him off at the emergency gate. They'd hold us responsible for his death or something. No way.'

" 'Good point. Hey, I'm stoked about this deal I made. When's the next party?'

" 'Next Thursday sounds great to me.'

" 'Hey, did you wash your hands? Don't want no dead man on me.' "

"I turned my head to the wall where I was curled up. Death was just another thing.

"Donna!" I cried, leaping up. "No one even mourned! Things just went on. The dead man was a good story, then poof, gone, nothing." I walked to the window. "So I lay there on the carpet for the longest time. 'No one really cares about anyone here,' I screamed. 'The only real thing is the drugs, the parties, and your own survival.'

"So these people were my family now, I had thought. If anything happens, I could count on them. Lies! For them no one is important. Whether someone dies or goes to jail, life simply goes on. As long as there's a place to stay, and drugs, no one is missed for more than a few minutes. *They love me here as much as I am loved at home*. The awareness was pain, incredibly bitter. Never again could I fool myself like this. These people had carelessly dumped a body off in front of a hospital and returned for an evening of fun—no tears from anyone. Lying there, I cried—more for myself than the guy."

"This wasn't your first experience with death was it?" Donna asked. Her eyes were soft and sad.

"So close, yes. And death was closer after that. One of the dancers in the club with me talked about being depressed for a long time, but no one listened. She was beautiful, popular at the clubs, and always had a boyfriend. No matter. She was always sad, unless she was on stage. There she was perfect. She was a great dancer and very sexy. But she never thought so. She saved her money to get her breasts enlarged. Why she thought she'd be happy if her body was different, I don't know. The next time I heard about her, she was dead. Suicide. Her surgery, breast enlargement, went bad; the cosmetic surgeon did a terrible job. The thing she thought would save her pushed her over the edge.

"The other girls talked about her for a few days, but then she, too, was forgotten. The club customers who favored her switched their attention onto other girls. Did she have a family? Did anyone tell them. Would they care? Who buried her? No one knew. No one cared."

I pounded my fist into my hand. "When you were with each other, it was like family, everyone so close. One big happy family. But walk out the door, die, or just disappear off the face of the earth, it was as if you never existed at all." I whirled around, forgotten hurt lumping in my throat.

"Donna, is that just the way life is? Is it?"

"No, that's not the way life is," her gentle voice was strong. "You have seen a very small part of life, of human nature. A part of life no one should experience." She got out of her chair and walked to where I stood by the window, my hands still clenched.

"Cheri, will you pray with me?"

My heart broke off its hook. Tears rushed to my eyes. I nodded. "There is nothing I want more."

"Dear Father, please show Cheri Your love. She has seen such ugly things in her life. Please show her the beauty of heaven, of Your love, Your mercy. I know You have drawn her to You. Let her feel that. Give her hope and the courage to heal, to trust in You. Send Your Holy Spirit to give her the wisdom and ability to listen to You. Thank You for all the promises You have given us, especially the promises that You will give us a new heart and a new mind to replace the old one that has been so damaged. Thank You, Lord."

"Donna, what did you mean about promises for a new heart?"

"In the Bible . . . wait here. Let me get a Bible and show you." She returned with a Bible in her hand.

"In Ezekiel 36:26, God promises this:" she flipped to the text. 'A new heart I will give you, and a new spirit I will put within you; and I will take out of your flesh the heart of stone and give you a heart of flesh. And I will put my spirit within you" (RSV).

A spring of liquid light welled up inside. These words were words of life, these words were mine, my only hope. *There is nothing, nothing in my own spirit salvageable. Nothing!*

Oh, God, give me this new heart, this new spirit. I must believe!

CHAPTER

22

I felt a sweet trickle seeping through my rotting soul, the warm sap of faith, hope, and love flowing, and filling, wild and new, inside me. Some of the dead weight of moldering darkness entombing me was ripped off, blinding me with rich, touchable, overwhelming light. My heart, freed from decaying numbness, frothed with wonder, my feet could float. *God, You love me? You love me! And more, You have always loved me. Love. Is this it? Unconditional, undeserved, and completely mine? Donna is real, her love is real! And there's more love where hers came from, more than I can dream.*

I stayed with Donna for a little more than a week. Starving for more, I wolfed down everything I could about God, Jesus, and the Holy Spirit, who would help me heal. I couldn't get enough. Everywhere I went, it seemed, God sent people to teach me. They couldn't know my need or see the role they played. Once I walked out to the mailbox and met a man who shared his view of God with me. We stood by the mailbox for three hours.

One of the most powerful things I learned was written by a woman in 1905. She wrote:

> Every man is free to choose what power he will have to rule over him. None have fallen so low, none are so vile, but that they can find deliverance in Christ. The demoniac, in place of prayer, could utter only the words of Satan; yet the heart's unspoken appeal was heard. No cry from a soul in need, though it fail of utterance in words, will be unheeded (*The Desire of Ages*, 258).

This was written for me. Wow! My chains melted from His love.

This Mary Magdalene Donna had told me about, who was she? Now her story made more sense. Remembering her, suddenly I was far away.

It was now or never. She had to find Him. Slipping into the crowded room lilting with fife and harp, Mary Magdalene snuck unnoticed behind the laughing guests, chatting and feasting in the torch-lighted banquet room. Why did He have to be in the center of the room? She approached him, her face guarded softly by her shawl. He was deep in conversation with a friend on his right, munching something, chuckling now and then.

Quietly, she knelt at his feet, her hands shaking. These feet, how well she knew them. In her mind, once again she was sprawled in the dust, clutching her thin blanket, wanting to die. A foot bashed her in the ribs and cold words, hard and accusing, surrounded her. Squinting open an eye, she saw the popular teacher standing near her. Red shame blurred her vision, followed by a blank wall of numbness. Death would be welcome. She waited for the verdict, waited for the crash of stones, and then . . . Refusing thought, she waited. The man said nothing, only scratched a bit in the dirt, writing something. *What?* His feet scuffed his scrawl out, and he wrote again. *Hurry up and kill me.* Time dragged by, and she shut her eyes. She opened them and saw those sandled feet beside her.

"Mary." A strong hand warmed her shoulder and gently opened her frozen fist. *What?*

"Mary, look up." *He knows my name? Don't ask me to look up. He'll shrink back in disgust.*

"Who condemns you? Look around."

Who? Why, who doesn't? Yes, even I do. She looked. The violent, scoffing men were gone. Only a kind face framed her sight. *Can this be real? He wants an answer. I have no words to say.* "No one, Lord."

"Neither do I. Go. Sin no more."

His eyes looked into her very soul, saw the black, but didn't shudder. His eyes looked past all the things she was and all she'd done. He found His child, innocent and scared. He didn't see the damaged waif she had become but the woman she was meant to be. He saw what she was capable of, strengthened by His love.

Her eyes refocused. At His feet once more, again she had no words to say. Cracking open her perfume, she poured it on His calloused feet, the fragrance lifting every eyebrow, filling every nose. Curious, judging eyes bored toward her throughout the room, but lifting blurry eyes, she saw His only.

"Cheri!" It was no longer Mary cracking her heart open at Jesus' feet, but me. It was me in the dust; it was His hand on my shoulder; it was His eyes reading my heart. He saw someone forgiven, someone capable of love, of good, of life. I wanted to whoop with joy.

Jesus knew everything about Mary, a prostitute, and still loved her. How I wished I could have talked with her, because there seemed few so equally excited about God. I wanted to scream, to cry, to sit down with someone who knew what a gift I had just been given. God loves me!

"Oh, you're just a new Christian," I heard some say. "That

feeling will wear off." But Mary Magdalene wouldn't say that. Neither could I.

Then there was the woman at the well who had been married five times and then was living with a man not her husband when she met Jesus. I understood her, her need to be loved and the choices she had made. I understood her life and knew she was emotionally dying or dead when she met Him. Like her, incredible joy rushed through me to realize this man is God, and He loves me. He loves me! I'm not only safe, but saved.

Rahab, a great-great-grandma of Jesus, gave her life to God while still a prostitute, working in the city of Jericho. Joseph's family, except for his father, hated Joseph. They plotted to kill him and sold him into slavery. David who killed a man because he was attracted to the man's wife, was still called a man after God's own heart. Story after story applied to me. But best of all, God sent His Son to die for us, to save us from ourselves and sin. Jesus promises that when God looks at me all He sees is His Son in all His glory. All heaven rejoiced when I accepted God into my life. And, too good but too true, He's coming back for me.

There was so much to learn. I had stopped thinking years ago, responding only to the situation I was in. Now I needed to learn to think again, to be aware of the time, what day it was, what month, and even what year. On the streets, the day didn't matter, only food, drugs, finding a place to sleep, and being safe.

After a week at Donna's, Jake and I returned to Long Beach and soon took a trip to Las Vegas.

"Will you marry me?" Jake asked me, over $5,000 we had just won in a game of Black Jack.

"Why not? Now?" He was a clean guy, stable and caring. With good looks and charm and a family like his, I couldn't be happier.

"Yes, here in Vegas." Laughing, we found a legal justice that night and married. Now I had a new husband for my new life. Tingly fingers of excitement ran up my spine, and also fear. There was so much I had to learn. Where could I start? Education.

When I went to take my GED test, I realized I couldn't read well enough to finish the test. What I could read, I didn't fully understand. The math section completely overwhelmed me. I did the only thing I could. Guess. Making a nice pattern on the answer sheet, I stuck to the C column most of the way. I was told that if I didn't know the answers to fill in C, and most of the time you will be right. Discouraged, I finished my test fast. How can I get an education if I can't even get into school because I can't pass this test?

Weeks later, I tore the envelope with the test score open. Surprise! I had passed.

I immediately signed up for a nursing program. It would be hard, due to the reading thing, but I bought a dictionary. The first semester I took anatomy and physiology and pharmacology. While I couldn't even pronounce the words, I poured over my dictionary. I didn't tell anyone of my illiteracy, that I had faked my GED, or that my emotions were incredibly damaged. But God was with me, a constant in my life.

"I'm too stupid to do this, God," I cried, often frustrated.

"Everything is all right, Cheri. You can do this," He answered. "Trust Me." *Trust?* For the first time, I could.

Now to find legitimate work. I couldn't work in bars and deal with all the pain, anger, and damage of that lifestyle. Not with Jesus in my life. In six months, I had nine jobs. I worked in sales, in health spas, at Denny's restaurant, and two dentist offices. In one dentist's office, I got some much-needed dental work. God's care amazed me.

I finally found a job I knew I could do and really loved. At Fairview State Hospital in Costa Mesa, California, I was trained to work with the developmentally disabled, on the Down's Syndrome unit. While I saw myself doing great things in this job, I had no clue why God had placed me here. But those who have worked with people having this disability will fully understand. The Lord placed me there because I needed to be loved, and these kids loved me to death. Once, returning to work after a long weekend off, the kids I worked with were so excited to see me that they stood up and clapped. It floored me. I can't wait to see them in heaven to thank them for all they gave me. Their unconditional love was water to my thirsty soul.

Sometimes I spent the entire shift teaching a group of young adults how to wash their faces, brush their teeth and hair. As I worked with them, God let me know He was working with me. *We're all at different levels in the learning process.* The thought made me smile.

And talk about learning. I went to school full time, worked full time, and was being held and healed by God full time. Amazement kept me bobbing up in wonder. I found one of Donna's churches in Costa Mesa and fell in love with the people there. I studied the Bible with a group of eleven new Christians, all enthused as I was. I couldn't get enough. Hope, like each new day, shot its warming rays, bright and glorious, into my life. For the first time, I loved getting up in the morning. It was a new day, full of surprises that only God knew would come. I loved my life.

"Come with me, Jake," I asked one morning getting ready for church. "You would really like it. I've got a great bunch of friends."

"Quit asking," Jake replied, watching TV. "That might work for my family and maybe for you, but it's not for me."

"But don't you feel empty without God? I can't imagine living without Him now."

"My life isn't so bad. I just don't feel a need for God. Come on, I don't want religion to take over our whole lives."

"But Jake, it's more than . . .

"Know what? You have become so boring since you got into this religion thing."

"But Jake, this is the best thing that's ever happened to me. I have never felt so alive, so involved with life, so good, ever! It's not something I just got into. Please understand. I have seen Him! I have experienced God for the first time in my life! I can't pretend it didn't happen and go back to my old life."

"But you have changed so much." He sighed.

"I know I have. Isn't that a good thing? I was a dancer in a club, a drug addict, and I hated life. I hated myself. How can I go back to that life? There's no way!"

"Go to your church. I don't want to talk about it anymore." He flipped off the TV and walked away.

One day I received a letter from Golden West College, my school. *What is it?* I wondered.

"Oh, my goodness! The Dean's list! Jake, I made the dean's list!"

"Big deal," Jake said, turning away.

"But it's me! Can't you understand?" I flipped out. "This means I'm not stupid. I do have value. I can succeed. I can change my life. No big deal? It's incredible! Thank You, God! This assurance was just what I've needed."

"You always get so worked up about things. Give me a break," he said as he walked to the door. "And God didn't do it. You did it!"

I could feel the distance between us widening. *Jake, don't go. Rejected and abandoned all my life, shouldn't I be used to this?* But after so much hope and love, his indifference stung, swelling purple poison through my heart. *You're my husband. I need you. The Bible says you are to represent Christ in our home. Ha! You don't even want Christ in our home, much less represent Him.*

I sank onto the living-room sofa, still clutching the dean's list. *Jake would love me to give God up, but that would kill me. If this relationship doesn't first.* Jake liked to rescue damaged women. When we first met, he did everything for me. He catered to me as if I were the only woman in the world. So messed up, I must have seemed a lifelong project. But God gave me a new heart, a new spirit, and a love that would heal me. *I don't need Jake to fix anything. I need him to be my husband.*

Jake returned from work the next day.

"I'm having fantasies about this sixteen-year-old girl I met at the bank."

"Really," I felt nauseous. "Does she work there?"

"Oh, she's a student volunteer. I just can't stop thinking about her."

"Why are you telling me this?"

"I thought it was only right. I don't want to keep secrets. She's a knockout and so funny. She has no idea how exciting she is."

"I don't know what to do. What should I do?" I asked, disbelieving and angry.

"Nothing. It's no big deal." He walked away.

Sometimes I tried to act damaged, as if I needed help. Then Jake would rush in to fix whatever the problem was. He'd also buy drugs, mostly pot or alcohol, to celebrate this or that. If I protested, he would pull away, growing cold.

"We need to get counseling," I pleaded.

"You need counseling. I am fine. I am no different than when you met me. You're the one who's changed. You definitely need a psychiatrist." He laughed. "I am the same yesterday, today, and tomorrow," using words from the Bible.

"I cannot go on like this . . . it's killing me emotionally. We have to do something."

"Are you threatening me?" he demanded.

"No."

"Because if you leave me, you will just end up on the streets again. You know that, don't you? I am the only reason you made it off the streets." He said that as if trying to be kind, but I only heard malice. *On the streets again* . . . . His words haunted me.

Was he right? Without him, would I end up on the streets again?

CHAPTER

23

The changes continued. Learning a whole new lifestyle, I had to give up smoking and a lot of other harmful habits and figure out how to replace them with healthy ones. Once I became so discouraged, I flung myself on my bed and began to cry.

"Lord, I can't do it. There is too much hurt and damage. I don't fit in anywhere. And Jake despises me. I don't know how to act, with him or anyone. Please help me."

Suddenly, a warm hand seemed to lift me high above all the worries and problems of this world. Was I awake or sleeping? I saw people, like ants, running frantically around without a purpose. *When in My love, while in the world, you are no longer a part of it*, I heard Him say. *You are discouraged and will be for a while, but know for sure that someday you are coming home to a place where you truly belong. You will fit in. Hang in there*. Peace filled me.

"God, You are for real," I sighed, knowing everything else was shadow.

Home remained a dark secret. I never had told anyone about my home life before, except Donna, and why start now. *Besides, the Bible says I should stay with my husband and pray, doesn't it? I must do the right thing. Why is it so hard?*

"Let's all be baptized at the same time," someone in my Bible study group suggested.

"Yes, let's," we all agreed. We were so close. We shared the common bond of trying to know God. Far from pretending to be perfect or having all the answers, we were just thrilled to be learning about love, forgiveness, who God is, and how much He loves us. With these friends only, could I truly relax.

We planned an entire service around our baptism. I don't know how common that was, but we all had a lot to say to our new family and to God.

"Let's do song service, too," someone suggested.

"Great idea. Can you sing?"

"No, but God doesn't care if we're off-key." None of us, out of eleven people, could sing. But nothing slowed us down, we warbled the hymns with all our hearts.

"Amazing grace . . ." The old hymn was gloriously new. *"How sweet the sound . . ."* The glad meaning pulsed through me. *"That saved a wretch like me . . ."* Through the missed notes and our tears, the church was touched.

Jake, why didn't you come? *"I once was lost . . ."* I wanted him to share this moment. Maybe then he'd see. Maybe then he'd understand and join me. *"But now I'm found . . ."* But God was there. I felt His presence so strongly that I couldn't think of the pain of Jake and our relationship. *"Was blind but now I see."* I couldn't even think of the pain of a lifetime of rejection, abandonment, molestation, drugs, or an education on the street. *Someday I will be with my Father in heaven, away from all the pain and damage that sin has brought into the world and into my life.* That thought soothed me.

I continued to study the Bible, sometimes with the group, sometimes on my own.

I finished the nursing program, a major accomplishment for

me. This particular program was typically very difficult. To stay in, I had to maintain 85 percent or higher on each "section." Sometimes I believed Jake was trying to sabotage my education, but I would just pray harder and try to love him. He never returned my love.

My mom had earned her Social Work degree and headed a volunteer program. I did some volunteer work as part of my own program, as well as helped with my mom's agency. Though our relationship hadn't changed, I had. At least, I was being healed. Perhaps no one could see that yet, but I could feel change rustling, stretching, deep inside me.

I received The Carnation Bowl Award for my volunteer work and a Volunteer of the Year Award. I gained a sense of self-worth from doing something good for my community. My whole life had been on the sidelines where people just took whatever they got their hands on. This was different. This felt right. Helping out gave me a sense of what God intended for us. The golden rule, "Do unto others what you would have them do unto you," played a central role in my healing, a part of the education I was receiving from my heavenly Father.

Finishing school, I had to take the state boards to get my nursing license. I was scared. I studied night and day. *Who do you think you're kidding?* my mind tormented me. *You will never pass this test. You can fool some of the people some of the time, but not . . ."*

I called my mom. I needed some reassurance.

"You have always been a con artist. You'll do fine."

What did she mean by that? I have always been a con artist? Did she think I conned my way through this nursing program? Did I? Doubts overwhelmed me. I looked to Jake for support. He sensed my vulnerability and moved in for the kill.

"God, help me!" My life teetered on the shaly brink of a vast gorge. I was slipping.

"Jake! I passed the state boards! I passed! I can't believe it. I have to celebrate."

Jake's support was superficial, and he quickly changed the subject. "You know that my mother's got cancer," Jake said. "We need to move to Sacramento to take care of her. She's dying."

"That bad off?"

I knew that Jake's mother had wanted to see him married before she died, and that was part of the reason he married me.

Soon, Jake lost all interest in me. He lost interest in life, but he denied that. He didn't go back to work for a year after our move to Sacramento, and when he did, he got a minimum-wage job at a dog kennel.

He denied that any of this bothered him.

" I am the same yesterday, today, and forever. You are the one who has changed."

I got a job working in a hospital on the mental-heath unit. I loved this job because most of the patients were so hopeless and I, with God, was full of hope. I knew that if God could change my life, He could change theirs. Only He could give them a hope and a future. I also worked with kids, sexual-abuse victims and recovering addicts. While I loved my work and my new lifestyle, my life reeled from the pain of Jake. When his mom died, he stopped trying altogether. He haunted cheap bars, run down ones, looking for someone else to rescue. Emotionally and physically he was pulling away from me. He would avoid intimacy for months at a time. I tried to get him to talk, to go to a counselor, or just talk with family members. Nothing seemed to work.

When I would blurt out, "I can't live like this!" he would would reply, "If you leave me, you will end up on the streets again!" Once, he went so far as to tell me that if I needed physical attention, I should get a lover. From the way he said it, I could tell that it wouldn't bother him at all.

I began to feel dead inside again. I couldn't even sense God's presence in my life anymore. Finally, I packed my bags and just moved out.

God, how could you do this to me? I hate you! I hit bottom.

CHAPTER 24

I need to take some time off from work," I told my supervisor at the hospital. "I just can't make it right now."

"We've enjoyed your working here for the past two years. Can't you work longer?"

"I'm sorry. Can I take a year's leave? I really have some things in my life to work out."

My supervisor looked sad. "Please come back as soon as you can. We want you here. I respect you and the job you do."

"Thanks." *I wish I could feel that way. But how could you know? If you knew the imposter I am . . .* I left.

Hope, turning deadweight, tore through my thin brown bag of faith, leaving empty despair to fill its space. I was back on the streets. So Jake was right. I was nothing, nothing but a drug addict. He doesn't love me. Who did I think I could fool? Yeah, I'm the biggest con artist ever. My mom was right. I trashed everything, my marriage, my hospital job, and my church. What was my religious experience worth anyway? I had flung away the only love I'd ever known, God. And He was through with me. Like stepping out of a sauna into icy air, the coldness bit more bitter than I had ever known. I did what I had done all my life and lost myself in the world of drugs.

A year passed. I let drugs, other people, and my familiar fear pin me once again. This time I didn't find the same relief. I missed God, and I missed the peace I'd known. But my chance had passed. I was lost in a big, empty dream, running. Nothing was real anymore.

"Cheri! It's you!" It was Diane, one of my friends from the study group who was baptized with me. She had found where I was staying. I don't know how. The apartment smelled of tobacco and dust. "Where have you been hiding?"

I reddened. Shame filled me, and I wanted to shrink. "I haven't been coming to church."

"I know! I've missed you! What happened?"

"I just can't do it. I thought I had something that no one could take away. I was so wrong. Now Jake is gone, my life is gone. Even God. I'm nothing. Who was I trying to fool?"

"Oh, Cheri!" Her concern was real. "Your education! Jake did not go to school for you. You have built yourself up, not Jake. Your accomplishments are real: dean's list, state boards, your hospital job, Volunteer of the Year Award, and more."

"But my relationship with God was posed. Look at me now. I have lost Him."

"No, Cheri. Your relationship with God was real. He's still here. Your change was real."

"My change? Look at me now. I'm back were I used to be, worthless."

"Cheri, you have only slipped and are scared. You are not a worthless nothing." She touched me warmly on the arm. "You are a child of God. Do not let this relationship, this Jake you loved, destroy the love you have now, the life you have now. Cheri, you can't!"

"How can I just come back to God? I don't know how. After

all I've done since I left Him, will He even want me back? There's no way." I couldn't hold my tears.

Diane sat beside me on the sagging sofa and held my hand. "Do you remember the story of the prodigal son?"

"What about it?"

"Christ told the story of this wasteful, runaway son, who had thrown God out, to teach us what God is really like. Like a Father, He waits with open-armed love to receive the returning prodigal boy, not even yelling accusations or insults at him. He doesn't even say 'I told you so.' Cheri, imagine it. God runs to meet you, yes, you, to bring you home. He then prepares a party to welcome you, his daughter, home where you belong. He loves you. He wants you with Him."

"But I've fallen so deep." I knew she was right. "How can I come back to Him?" My forehead crinkled.

"It won't be easy. Do you think for a second that Satan will let up on you while you're discouraged? He's got you where he wants you, and he'll fight to keep you. But God is fighting to get you back. And He is stronger."

"But I'm such a failure. And, good grief, everyone I've ever trusted has let me down."

"Cheri, we're all failures. If everyone fails you, and if you fail everyone, you can still rely on God. You mustn't look to others for security, only Jesus. Other people at times will be helpful, and others will be extremely hurtful, Cheri. Only God is safe!"

Donna's words echoed in my mind. *You can't trust me. People will always let you down.*

"We are all damaged. You're not the only one in the world," Diane continued. "God says even the best of us are damaged by sin and need a Saviour to restore us to God. To teach us to love."

I blinked at Diane. *God, did you send her to me? You did, didn't You? And I can see Your arms out right now, wanting me, loving me, forgiving me. Oh, God. I'm sorry! I'm coming home. And that's only where You are. With You only am I safe.*

"Will you pray with me?" I whispered. We prayed, she hugged me, and left. A song, something like a meadowlark's, warbled in my heart.

I looked at myself in the mirror. My long blond hair was disheveled, and circles purpled under my eyes. What a mess. I had to start taking care of myself again. I had to kick these drugs again and quit my smoking. But I needed help. Going back to church, I asked them for help. I was told that if a member smoked a cigarette, they would be disfellowshiped. *What? I needed acceptance, and I needed help to stop! Come on!* I left the church again, angry at their ignorance, hurt by their rejection.

"God, I need help. Can no one see that? I can't make it alone," I prayed.

"*I'm with you, Cheri.*" I heard Him say. "*We're going to make it. It's Me and you now. Us. Are you ready?*"

"Yes, Lord. I give up. I'm helpless on my own."

"*I am glad that you finally see that. Come on, I've got a lot to teach you.*" I couldn't see Him, but I knew He held my hand.

God and I began again the journey of our life, together. He taught me first how to forgive myself, how to forgive the church, and how to forgive my family. Even how to forgive Him. It was a new relationship here, with lots of ups and downs, and I couldn't always agree with His methods at first. He led me to friends and counselors who helped me explore my abandonment issues, my fear of being alone, and helped me discover who I was, apart from all the damage. Like paddling up some rocky rapids, it was both exhilarating and extremely hard work.

I had to challenge all my beliefs. With so many irrational beliefs about myself, about others, life and God, it is a wonder I'd been able to hear God at all. I fell deeply in love with Him. How patient He was and still is with me.

Now that I was back, I had to start to dress right, act right, eat right, and live right. But how? I studied how other women dressed, and I copied them, practicing also how they talked, acted, and ate. I took seminars and workshops on how to act, dress, eat, behave, and even how to witness for God. Overwhelmed, I broke down again.

"Jesus," I cried. "This is too hard. It's not for me. I can't stand lace dresses and these frilly fashions. I'm dying for junk food. I just don't fit in. And I really want a cigarette." I kept praying. "Please, God, You can make me want to dress and act like everyone else. I need to be like them. Help me be a Christian. You've got to help me fit in." I knelt, pleading. Only silence.

A memory filled my mind, vivid and ugly. I was back in a drug house on the bathroom floor, overdosed on heroin. I had stopped breathing and lost control of my bowel and bladder. Several people, other addicts, tried to bring me back to life. First, they dragged me into the shower and turned on the cold water. That failed, so they removed my clothes. "Can someone do CPR?" someone yelled. "Get some ice from the kitchen," another yelled. Someone ran to the kitchen and brought back ice cubes. They placed ice cubes in my mouth and around me. I don't know how, but somehow that worked, and I gasped, breathing again.

What, God? What's the point of this bad memory? I groaned. His voice filled my mind.

"I loved you when you were lying on the bathroom floor, overdosed on heroin, lying in your own waste. I love you now. My love is not conditional. My love is not given only when you behave or look good enough or when you turn into a Christian or when you think you look and act like one. I have always loved you. I will always love you."

I was stunned. That's incredible! Where did He come from? How could I ever show my gratefulness? *Lord, teach me how to stand firm in Your love! No matter what is happening to me or around me.* It hit me that most people think of God the way I had started to. That He loved us only when we behaved and acted as "Christians."

That thinking is bad news, because we never really behave. We don't know how. God says that even our very best is like filthy rags. The good news is that God teaches us how to grow spiritually through His love. The best news is I become more like God as I am drawn by His love, and in His love I am changed into His image. What a promise!

As I was first joining the church, I had met a spiritual leader in the church with an incredible ministry, wonderful family, and knowledgeable about everything spiritual. I'd listen to him for hours, spending more time at the university where he taught so I'd gain more insight into God, Jesus, and the Holy Spirit. Remembering him, I asked around for him.

"He left his wife and family and the church," they told me. "He doesn't even know if he still believes in God."

"Impossible! How could that happen?" I wanted to call him up. Could I help in some way? He had helped me without even knowing it. If he could fall, any of us could. Talking with someone who knew him well, it struck me. Where before he'd been a saint, everyone now saw him only as a sinner, one outside the circle.

Bad news. He was always a sinner, a sinner in need of a Saviour. But the good: even now he has one, Jesus, waiting for him to come back like the prodigal son. Jesus longs to give him rest in God's love, relieve his suffering, replace his spiritual poverty with riches from a Father who wants to celebrate his return with a festival. I pray for his return.

God, through this man's tragedy, showed me again how our view of God's love can interfere with our ability to trust Him. I can't see God as someone who accepts me only when I am good enough, because I need Him most when I fail miserably. I need him most when I lose my way.

"Neither death, nor life, nor angels, nor principalities, nor powers, nor things present, nor things to come, nor height, nor depth, nor any other creature, shall be able to separate us from the love of God, which is in Christ Jesus our Lord" (Romans 8:38, 39).

This is the surgery that will heal my heart. And I don't want a Band-Aid.

I finally learned, no matter what, that God is with me for the long haul. He will walk with me, teach me, even if it's how to walk in the first place. He will put up with my irrational thinking and behavior until I can, through His love, give them up. He will not abandon me. He will do everything He can to keep me close. Such is His love, head over heels. And I'm in love.

Now I had to face another truth.

CHAPTER

25

Loneliness clung to me like damp clothes in an early-morning chill. I shivered. *God*, I cried, *I trust You. But why does it hurt? I thought if I trusted You, I wouldn't be afraid of being alone.* I gazed out at my lawn. For the first time in my life, I rented an apartment all by myself. A sparse patch of grass out front nestled a picnic bench and two small beach chairs. A green spider plant, scrawny and struggling, grew in a tiny clay pot.

If I can learn to trust You, I won't be afraid, right? I won't need someone to rescue me. I opened the screen door and stepped out into my little yard. The air smelled cool, and a breeze brushed lightly on my skin. Here in my tiny haven, I forgot I lived in a smelly part of town and that only a small fence kept the peace inside from straying. I sat down, burying my face in my hands. *What's wrong with me? On my own, just God and me, it will be fine. I can take care of myself. I don't need Jake or anyone to shelter me. I'm OK.* I looked up at the empty sky, bigger, somehow, than I'd ever remembered. My eyes passed over the fence to the street in front. It seemed a world away.

The Cheri Peters Story

Like a small mouse chewing at night in a big house, the truth gnawed on me. *My God, I'm dying. I can't look.* I went into the house and brought out a cup of water for my little plant. It was brave and holding its own, but it hadn't grown a bit since I'd bought it.

"*You have to look, Cheri. Ignoring it won't make it go away.*"

"*OK.*" Bracing myself, I turned, looking my fear fully in the face. I shuddered at what I saw.

My life was but dark survival between men. Could I live without them? Now I was alone.

Come on! So what, I thought. *Many people are alone. It's no big deal.* But I couldn't shake the terror that landed on me. I had always relied on some man to take care of me.

Now I saw it. Afraid of being alone and rejected, I took abuse in exchange for the supposed security. Drugs had blocked my view of all my fears and insecurities. The more drugs I used, the poorer my judgment was; the poorer my judgment, the more perpetrators and addicts would move into my life *to take care of me.* Leaving Jake forced me to look at my long-nursed fears. I'd been oblivious. I hadn't given up my psychological bondage during our seven-year marriage. I stared at my life, mouse-chewed and moldy.

"Life doesn't have to be like this," I cried. "God, show me whatever I need to see in order to be whole," I prayed. "I want to respond to my environment and people around me in a healthier way, with love. Help me! What do I do?"

"*Rely on Me alone.*"

"But I don't know how to, God. What does that mean?"

"*Try no relationships for one year.*"

My palms began to sweat. *I don't know how to act outside a relationship. I have always just responded to people in my life and never thought for myself.*

"*Think for yourself.*"

I gasped, surprised. "But who am I? I'm a mystery. God, can't you just fix me?"

"*I will get you through.*"

I sighed. This wasn't going to be easy. Who was I, anyway? It was easier going back to school, learning to read, and finding a job than it was exploring and challenging my irrational self. Socially underdeveloped, I had no idea what my interests were outside of work. *Am I really nothing inside? Am I a fraud?*

I looked at my scraggly spider plant and smiled.

God promised. He would get me through.

No longer could I waste time. Starting work again at the American River Hospital in Sacramento, I loved my unit, the people, and the counseling I did. As soon as I'd learn something, I'd practice it and teach it to others. Teaching was the best way to learn, I'd heard. It was true for me. During my relapse, I realized even more the importance of dealing with my issues, of learning new ways to live, to communicate, and to take care of myself. Recovery spurted through a thicker vein this time, a deeper level.

Standing in a K Mart in the household appliance section, I fingered a shiny set of silverware. Mine. I bought it with my first paycheck. The shiny metal gleamed as I washed and placed the silverware neatly in my kitchen drawer. My own set, my very own! I started crying. Though it was an inexpensive set, to me it meant a new life.

"What did I always want to do as a child?" I asked myself. The answer was instant: piano lessons. I would have learned to play and read music. Renting a small piano for nineteen dollars a month, I began to practice. I loved sitting at the piano, counting a beat, and holding my fingers poised and curled over the ivory keys. Going to piano lessons and hearing all the children doing so well while I still fumbled through my scales made me envious, but I loved learning.

I thanked God for teaching me to play not only piano, but just how to *play*, to enjoy my leisure time. I thanked Him for helping me discover what I can do, what my interests are, and my physical, emotional, and spiritual gifts as well.

I took a tennis class. I loved it! Excited, I joined a group of people who played tennis in a tournament. I had a woman partner for doubles who was an excellent player. We both were.

Through learning what I liked to do and developing skill, I was learning who I was. Not just a recovering addict, a woman from the streets, or a victim of child abuse, I was a woman of God. For the first time, I enjoyed my time alone, enjoyed learning to play and to live.

My spider plant was growing.

"Hey, Cheri," my new friend Debbie, a fund-raiser for the Sacramento Symphony, said, "Would you like to come to a symphony performance with me this Saturday night?"

"Me? Wow! Of course I would." I had never listened to classical music, other than the piano pieces I was learning. But people had to struggle to even recognize that. "When does it start?" *What should I wear? Me at a symphony? I can't believe it.*

"It starts at 7:30. I'll come over, and we'll head out from your place."

I had nothing to wear for a symphony, so I bought a new silk evening gown. Slipping into its soft elegance for the evening, I couldn't believe it was me. I checked the mirror. There was someone new in there who smiled at me, her fair skin rosy. *Like Cinderella! Who will believe where I'm going now? A symphony concert! I wish my old friends could experience something this wonderful. Stop thinking of the past, Cheri,* I told myself. *Live now!*

I looked at my watch. 7:10. *Where is Debbie?* I paced the apartment. 7:15. *She couldn't have forgotten. Where in the world was she?*

A horn tooted, and I dashed out the door.

"Sorry I'm late," Debbie said, frazzled. She was wearing a red lace-trimmed dress. "If we arrive late, they won't let us in.

No one gets seated after the concert begins because it's too disruptive."

"Hurry then! It's 7:20 right now! We can't miss this!" She stepped on the gas.

7:35. We pulled into the crowded concert hall parking lot.

"What are we going to do? I don't want to miss the first half," I said. Disappointment caught in my voice. We parked and hurried over to the front entrance. It was closed.

"No!" I wailed. "Don't tell me this."

"*Hmmm*," Debbie's forehead furrowed. "Hey, don't worry. Let's sneak in through the back entrance."

"What? We'll get caught! We can't just sneak in. That's illegal."

"It's OK. Follow me. We'll just go through the back and sit down."

"Well, we already have our tickets. I'm not missing this."

"Come on," she urged, running in her heels toward the back entrance. I followed. Turning the corner, we saw two men dressed in tuxedos lounging on a bench outside the back door.

"Great. We can't sneak in now," I whispered.

"It's OK."

"But what if . . ."

"Hi, Debbie," one of the men said. *She knows these guys?*

"Hi, Steve! What are you two doing out here still? Isn't the concert about to start?"

"We don't play this first half. We're getting fresh air," the other man said. "Who's your friend?" He smiled.

"Cheri, this is Brad and Steve. They both play trumpet in the symphony. Listen," she turned to them. "We've got a problem. We're late, obviously, and now we can't get in. Can we sneak in this back way?"

"No problem." Brad winked at me.

"Hey, Debbie, it's my birthday today," Steve said. "We're celebrating after the concert. Why don't you and Cheri join us?"

"That'd be great!" Debbie exclaimed.

"Just come over to the Hyatt Regency, and we will see you there after the concert," Steve said, his grin widening. He opened the door and called to the security guard. "These are our friends. It's OK if they go backstage. They were running late."

Laughing, Debbie and I followed the guard. I felt even more like Cinderella.

The guard led us to a side door that opened toward the front. We slid into two red cushioned chairs and sighed with relief. Just in time.

The music floated, pulling, coaxing, lifting my spirits. I had never seen or heard so many instruments playing together in one place. The instruments talked to each other, questioning, murmuring, answering, soaring. I sat in awe, the music a surge around me. One piece, heavy and mysterious, was twilight fading into dark. It was discouragement and heartache. I could relate. The next piece was light and flutey, a sunrise and a spiritual awakening. The energy of both pieces, though vastly different, held me spellbound. The music faded.

"Cheri. Cheri!" Debbie nudged me. "It's over." The house lights came on.

"I could listen to this music all night," I sighed. "It's over far too fast."

"I know. Isn't it? But the evening's far from over. Let's head over to that party at the Hyatt."

"Oh, Debbie, do we have to? I don't know anyone."

"Sure you do. Brad and Steve. I'll introduce you to some other friends. It'll be fun." Debbie steered me out of the concert hall to the glittering night outside. "Some trivia for you. Brad is Mr. December on Sacramento's Most Eligible Bachelor's Calendar. Isn't that a trip?"

"He's on a calendar?" I laughed. "I can see why." We entered the Hyatt and found the large hall complete with a small stage, chairs, and large dancing floor. Within a few minutes, the place filled with orchestra players, all in black-and-white tuxedos or evening wear. I gulped. *I don't belong here.* Debbie spotted a few of her friends and introduced me to them. I smiled and nodded and tried to say a few pleasantries. Black and white and shiny colors mingled around me. Wandering away from Debbie and her social clique, I looked for a quiet corner.

I tucked myself into a soft chair and watched. Laughter and camaraderie drifted around me, but in the formal air, I squirmed. *I don't belong here.* Two men in tuxes sat down near me.

"Can you believe we had to play that piece again?"

"I know. I've played that piece so many times, I could play it in my sleep."

"Thank God it's only scheduled one more week."

"I thought it was incredible," I burst out. I couldn't help it. Their eyebrows lifted. "I have never heard it before. I was so moved, and I hoped the piece would never end."

They looked at each other, then at me. With a quick laugh, I turned away, wanting to disappear into the crack of my chair. *They must think I'm crazy. They can't know my background. How would they know how this music, this night, has touched me? They can't know that it is only by the grace of God that I am here!* I sighed. *Thank You, Lord,* I whispered.

A small band set up on stage and started playing. I leaned forward, intently listening to the saxophone and trumpet. Jazz now, it was hard to keep my feet from tapping. *There's Mr. December,* I mused. He was playing his trumpet, and very well. His forehead shone soft with perspiration.

I couldn't help but notice him. He was tall, broad-shouldered, and handsome. His dark, wavy chocolate hair, strong bearded chin, and playful expression captured my attention. Resting his mouth, he looked out, his brown eyes catching mine and twinkling recognition. I half smiled back and glanced away at the other players. Casually returning my eyes to him, something tickled right out of my skin. He was still watching me. His smile flashed beneath his mustache. I glanced to see if there was someone else behind me. No.

Oh, help. My heart skipped a couple beats, then raced to catch up. I looked around for Debbie. *I think I'm ready to go now.* My knees trembled. I couldn't see her.

Maybe I should just wander over to that group of people there. I felt sick. *I think I'll just find the restroom.* I couldn't move. *No relationships. No men. I can't trust my judgment. Good grief. I can't even trust myself to talk to him.* As I sat there trying to decide what to do, the song ended. Another one began. *Maybe he just smiles at everybody.*

"Hi. Would you like to dance?" My heart jumped right into my throat. Brad had left the stage, meandered my way, and now stood beside me, comfortable, smiling, and expectant.

"Uh, sure." What else could I do?

"Wow. You sure know how to dance," I said, fascinated by his fancy footwork. I was tripping all over myself.

"You're the first person I've tried out my new footwork on."

"Ever?"

"Dance lessons. I'm quite the klutz." He wasn't in a million years. I laughed.

We danced and laughed the rest of the evening. I forgot my fear.

"Hey, you have some free time this week?"

Oh no! "I'm not in a place to even date," I told him, turning red.

He smiled. "No problem. But you should really join this dance class with me. I need a partner."

I relaxed. We'd be friends. I not only joined his class, but taught him to play tennis. He taught me to play golf. We both loved sports, so we played together a lot. *What a fun guy!* I thought. *But, no, we could never date. We're from too different backgrounds. Two different worlds!*

That's out of the question.

Brad's family, warm and loving, were involved in every aspect of his life. They played, worked, achieved goals, camped, and loved each other. I'd laugh at the stories of the "bad" things he did, like throw snowballs at people from the school roof. He was so cute.

He would tear up when he heard stories of my childhood or my life. He encouraged me when I had to work through yet another issue. When I was back in school full time earning my teaching degree, Brad let me write my term papers on his computer.

I started to miss him when he didn't call.

When he came over to my apartment to pick me up, he would play on the piano while I finished getting ready. I'd be chronically late. His playing was different from mine. He even used both hands. Sometimes I'd just sit down in my room and listen. I enjoyed the feelings I had when he was around. What a good *friend*.

"Someone's been hanging out behind my apartment every night," I told Brad one day. "You have a Peeping Tom?"

"I think so. It's rather annoying. No big deal, really."

"No big deal, my foot! If I ever see him, I'll beat the tar out of him."

"I'm OK."

"If anything happens to you, Cheri, . . ." Brad touched my hand. He was very protective. He made excuses for coming over more. He reminded me to shut my curtains at night and lock the doors.

We fell in love.

Now we both had to look hard at this reality. We talked for hours about our goals, our dreams, and our families. If we were to get married, his family would be mine, mine would be his. As wonderful as Brad was, that was hard for him to accept. Brad would have to meet my family before he could make a well-informed decision. Was accepting my family too much to ask? I had to know, even if it killed me.

CHAPTER 26

I took Brad home for Christmas. My family was deep into partying when we arrived. My youngest sister was high on crank. She weighed 79 pounds, and her teeth were rotted from crank. My step-father smoked pot with my brother-in-law, and my sister had snorted cocaine and was drinking vodka with orange juice. My other sister, Becky, showed up with more drugs. She was still dancing in bars and into cocaine.

I watched Brad as he watched them. *What is he thinking? I won't blame him at all if he can't handle this. How could I expect Brad to accept this into his life?*

On our way back to Sacramento, Brad looked at me. "Are you sure you weren't adopted?"

We both laughed.

The rest is history.

We were married. We have a beautiful daughter who has had such a loving family and home environment that I cry in gratitude to God. Every bit of the normal, everyday stuff thrills me more than I can possibly say. My family's unbelievable.

God has continued to teach me to trust Him. Many times he teaches me through Brad and Jacqi, my new family. But no matter how He chooses to teach me or how resistive I am, God is always gentle and persistent. I am His child.

I have spent years healing from my past. God has been so good to me. He has given me "hope and a future" (Jer. 29:11, NIV).

God has given me a new life. I am married to a wonderful man, and I have a beautiful child. I am an Art Therapist in a local hospital and work with high-risk kids through the school district. I am a well-respected member of our community. People are shocked when they learn of my history. They would never have guessed that I came from such a rough background.

Brad, my husband, knows everything about my past and still loves me. He is from an upper middle–class family. His father, now retired, was an engineer and at one time represented the United States Government in Bangladesh as an advisor and ambassador. His mother is a classical violinist in a symphony orchestra.

Brad remains a classical musician for a symphony orchestra, a fabulous husband, and a good father. He is very supportive of me and my growth. He says he understands the things in my background but has never known me as that person. He met me ten years into my recovery.

When asked to give my personal testimony at church, I wasn't sure I could do that. If I told everyone all this garbage, they might not like me. I didn't have a wonderful story. It isn't like I trained for the Olympics and won a gold medal. Fear squeezed me in its well-known vise.

"God, why are testimonies important, anyway?" I asked Him. "Why do people have to share? There is nothing good about my character to talk about."

"*It's not about your character, Cheri. It's about Mine.*"

"What?"

It's about the vindication of My character. When you give your testimony, it is to share with others the fact that I love them, that I am still very active in their lives."

Some think a changed life is no big deal. I can't believe that. A changed life is the most amazing thing there is. To take someone who was so damaged that she could not even see any reason to live and give her love for life—that is an amazing, wonderful, unbelievable thing.

After that, I counted it a privilege to give a testimony about my God. *But first,* I thought, *I need to do some research on not judging others so I can present that first. Maybe if I do that I will be judged less. It will be easier.*

I spent eight hours looking up everything I could about not judging others. I found some great texts in the Bible and quotes by famous authors that would bring second thoughts to anyone who even thought about judging others, especially me, when I would give my testimony.

Then God tapped me on the shoulder.

"Now that you have all this information together, Cheri, please study it."

"What? Why should I study it? I'm not the one with the . . ." Then I understood.

I was the one doing the judging. I was judging those in the church, accusing them of judging me. Another lesson learned.

"I'm sorry, Lord." I had pages of stuff. I really was judging them, and if I continued to do that, I would not be able to share God's testimony with them because of that sin. God makes me smile when He shows me my faults in such a humorous way. He has an incredible sense of humor.

"Lord, please give me the courage and words to present this testimony," I prayed. In my prayers, I constantly used homeless in the past tense. God shared a thought that has changed my life forever.

A MIRACLE FROM THE STREETS

I am still "homeless." This world is not my home. God showed me that we all live, spiritually speaking, in our cardboard boxes, some fancier than others, and if life is only about how many things we have in our shopping carts, then we will remain homeless, or as Jesus observed, "wretched, miserable, poor, blind, and naked."

He taught me that Jesus will come back someday and take me home. Until then, I can't expect things to be easy. We can't be surprised when tragedy strikes. If things are difficult here, it is because we are homeless. This is not our home. We will be home soon, but if we try to make this world our home, we will forever be frustrated.

This was my testimony: One, that God changes lives, an incredible miracle; and two, He is coming to take us home. We are all homeless.

The pastor knew I wanted to be rebaptized, so he arranged for my baptism on the same day as my testimony. That morning was perfect. My hair turned out just right, my clothes felt great. I sighed. Anticipation, not nervousness, tingled me as I drove to church.

"Cheri, we are going to do the baptisms first. Then you can give your testimony."

"Great."

The baptism was beautiful. I felt God's presence with me in the baptismal pool. Brad performed a wonderful piece on the trumpet. Then he was asked to speak. He walked up to the podium.

"Roses are red. Violets are blue. You're getting wet, 'cause God loves you."

I laughed. Everyone laughed. When the laughter died, he spoke of his love for me, of how God brought me into his life, and how much God means to us. It was wonderful—perfect.

Everything was perfect until I got back to the dressing room and realized that I did not bring a hair dryer, a brush, or a towel.

Good grief.

OK, now what am I supposed to be learning? I thought, sarcasm thick.

"This testimony is about Me, not you."

A lesson in vanity, now? Great.

Tap. Tap.

"Cheri, are you just about ready?"

It was the pastor. "Yes. Do you have a comb?"

"Sure."

I combed my hair, dried it as much as I could with a paper towel, dressed, and walked up on the platform. I took a deep breath. "God, help me remember that my case is settled. This is about You and Your character, not me. Jesus settled the issue about me and my character with His life and death." I began to speak.

I was amazed at the effect. After I finished speaking, people came by to shake hands. Some cried and talked about loved ones who were involved with drugs or others who were sexually molested and couldn't get beyond the damage. Everyone seemed touched at some level. A few people talked about feeling that God could use them to help others and that they wanted to learn to make a difference.

The comments and tears never seemed to end.

"Hello, Cheri. You do not know me, but my name is Gary Curry. I just wanted to tell you that I know Donna. In fact, I just heard her testimony a month or so ago."

"What? Donna? Her testimony?"

"Yes, she talked about a girl from the streets who taught her to love 'unconditionally.' She now has a jail ministry and works with addicts." He smiled and walked away.

"Did you hear that?" I looked at Pastor Stan.

"I did!"

"It is as if God was giving me a gift." I smiled.

The line of people continued to file past me. I wanted to find

Gary Curry and ask him to tell me more. Donna was touched by me as much as I was touched by her. Another lesson. God heals all those involved if we will only let Him. *I love You, Lord!*

"*Cheri.*" God's voice filled my mind. "*I want you to meet your true family.*"

"*What?*" I wanted everyone to be quiet for a minute. *My family? Where?* A girl walked up to me, shook my hand, and began to try to make sense of all her pain. The tears on my cheeks were joy. I knew.

I finally do belong.

This was my family. God is my Father, you my sister, my brother.

I am safe.

I, because of the things God is teaching me and the testimony He has given me, can give hope to others. My life, once so ugly and black, is now exciting and full. The life I have now is based only on the faith I have in God's love and promises.

I wish I could say that life now is always easy, that my new family is always loving. That they always do the right thing. That I always do the right thing. That I never feel pain or cause anyone else to feel it. I wish I could say everything is perfect now, but I can't. I still feel fear.

The fear of changing lifestyles, of entering a culture I knew nothing about (and did not trust) was incredibly significant. Once inside the church again, I realized I was no different than before. I was still homeless, surrounded by hurtful situations, seeing people horribly abuse themselves and each other. The only thing that remained, after my illusion was stripped away, was Jesus. He is the only reality. The only thing that stays.

I am happier now than I have ever been. I see God at work in people's lives every day. I know that one day soon, all the pain, illness, abuse, addictions, fear, hatred, all this sin and burning tears will be a bad memory. One day soon I will look into the eyes of God, and hear Him say, "I love you. Welcome home."